SMOKE
✬ AND ✬
FLAMES

SMOKE ★AND★ FLAMES

A DELICIOUS COLLECTION OF BARBECUE RECIPES

LOVE FOOD™

This edition published by Parragon Books Ltd in 2015
LOVE FOOD is an imprint of Parragon Books Ltd

Parragon Books Ltd
Chartist House
15—17 Trim Street
Bath BA1 1HA, UK
www.parragon.com/lovefood

ISBN 978-1-4723-7366-3

Printed in China

New recipes and home economy by Lincoln Jefferson
New photography by Mike Cooper
New text by Robin Donovan
Edited and project managed by Cheryl Warner
Designed by Lexi L'Esteve
Illustrations by Scott Rhodes, courtesy of The Bright Agency

Notes for the Reader
This book uses both metric and imperial measurements. Follow the same units of
measurement throughout; do not mix metric and imperial. All spoon measurements
are level: teaspoons are assumed to be 5 ml, and tablespoons are assumed to be
15 ml. Unless otherwise stated, milk is assumed to be full fat, eggs and individual
vegetables are medium, and pepper is freshly ground black pepper. Unless otherwise
stated, all root vegetables should be peeled prior to using.

Garnishes, decorations and serving suggestions are all optional and not necessarily
included in the recipe ingredients or method. The times given are an approximate
guide only. Preparation times differ according to the techniques used by different
people and the cooking times may also vary from those given. Optional ingredients,
variations or serving suggestions have not been included in the time calculations.

Contents

Bring on The Barbecue!

Food and fire combine to create one of the best things in life —
barbecue. Add a patio full of friends, a pair of barbecue tongs
in one hand and a cold beer in the other, and it doesn't get much
better. Grilling food — meat, veggies, even seafood or fruit — over
hot coals brings a deep, primal sense of satisfaction and pleasure.
And nothing brings out the natural flavours of meat and vegetables
quite the way cooking them on the grill does — whether using a high-
heat, fast-grilling method, low-and-slow cooking or smoking. Not to
mention, barbecuing is fast, delicious and easy to clean up.

A GRILL FOR EVERY PERSON, PLACE AND OCCASION

The array of grills on the market these days is mind-boggling — gas,
charcoal, electric, gigantic or small enough to carry to the beach. Whether
you opt for a full-sized charcoal grill, a balcony-sized electric grill or a
quick-cleaning gas grill is a personal choice and depends on your barbecuing
priorities. Whether you want intense smoky flavour or a system that will
allow you to cook up a delicious and healthy meal any place, any time, there
is a grill that is just right.

CHARCOAL, WOOD OR GAS?

If it's smoky, chargrilled flavour that draws you to barbecuing, a charcoal
or wood grill is your best bet. If, however, convenience, speed and easy
clean-up are most important to you, a gas grill cannot be beaten. The
recipes in this book are designed to be cooked on any of these types of
grills so whichever you decide, you can't go wrong.

CHARCOAL GRILLS AND KETTLES

Charcoal grills come in many shapes and sizes. The kettle grill is the
standard-style grill. Round with a deep bowl, a kettle grill has a grate
in the bottom that the charcoal sits on and, above that, a grill where the
food is cooked. Simple and functional, this type of grill is the perfect
solution for the frequent or occasional barbecue cook because it is sturdy,
inexpensive and versatile. You can use a kettle grill for high-heat
grilling, slower indirect cooking (what's known in grilling circles as true
barbecuing), and even as a smoker.

Charcoal grills also come in small, portable tabletop versions, as well as
large rectangular versions. Whichever you choose, look for one with sturdy
legs and adjustable vents that give you the ability to control the heat of
your fire.

Charcoal briquettes, which are manufactured from wood by-products, are easy to find (they're available in pretty much any supermarket), inexpensive and easy to transport, making them perhaps more convenient than wood. Easy-light varieties make using charcoal more convenient than ever — with these, you won't even need lighter fluid.

Lump charcoal, on the other hand, is a more natural form of charcoal. To make it, logs are burned in an oxygen-free environment and they are generally made without a lot of additives (meaning you won't get even a hint of lighter fluid's flavour in your food), leading purists to choose them over briquettes.

WOOD-FIRED GRILLS

Charcoal grills can also be used as wood-fired barbecues. The appeal of grilling over wood is that it adds flavour and, many think, is less polluting than charcoal. You can buy bags of wood chips and/or large hunks of various types of wood. Wood can be a lot more finicky than charcoal to cook with as you have to contend with many different factors — such as how dry the wood is or how big the pieces are, both of which affect how hot or fast they burn, how much smoke they put out, and what flavour they impart (for more on types of wood, see page 212).

Pellet grills use small pellets made by compressing sawdust, rather than whole pieces of wood. These pellets come in a variety of 'flavours' and burn cleanly and quickly to a fine ash. The small size and easy-to-control burn of the pellets means that these types of grills offer the best of both worlds. You get ease of use and convenience similar to a gas grill with the added smoky flavour of a hardwood grilling.

GAS GRILLS

Gas grills are ideal for people who want to be able to cook up a meal quickly and enjoy minimal clean-up. The biggest benefits of gas grills are that they heat up in minutes with the turn of a dial, have easily controlled heat, clean up easily, and are less polluting than charcoal. The downside of gas grills is that they don't work well for smoking and don't impart that delectable smoky, chargrilled flavour. Some barbecue purists turn their noses up at gas grills, but they are practical.

Like charcoal grills, gas grills come in a wide range of styles from small portable models to gigantic garden behemoths capable of grilling up meals for a crowd. Whichever size of gas grill you choose, go for the best quality you can afford.

Having multiple burners, too, is key to being able to control your heat and have versatility in your cooking abilities. Having two burners allows you to use both direct and indirect heat. Having three or more burners gives you even more heat control. Angled metal plates over the burners keep the heat evenly dispersed and prevent flare-ups. If you want to combine both the convenience of a gas grill with the smoky flavour-imparting abilities of a charcoal one, look for a gas grill with lava rocks. These are hard to find and more expensive, but if you're handy, you might be able to rig a standard gas grill to get the same effect.

ELECTRIC GRILLS

A new breed of outdoor electric grills has hit the market in recent years, opening up barbecuing possibilities for even those with no outdoor space save a small balcony or patio. While they don't have the power of either charcoal or gas, if it's your only choice, it will certainly do.

SMOKERS

To make delicious smoked meats, really all you need is a basic charcoal grill, but if you want to really impress your friends, some additional equipment is needed. Fortunately, there are plenty of stand-alone smokers and smoker attachments to choose from. With these, you can produce fantastic smoked foods without having to hover over the machine all day checking and adjusting the temperature, adding wood chips, or basting the meat. A good smoker or smoker attachment lets you set it and forget it and still put a great tasting meal on the table at the end of the day. You can also adapt charcoal, gas and electric grills for smoking (see right).

SMOKER ATTACHMENTS

The simplest way to equip yourself for barbecue smoking is a smoker attachment that extends the abilities of the grill you already have. If you've got a kettle grill, for instance, you can probably buy an inexpensive attachment that will virtually turn it into a stand-alone smoker.

Many gas grills can be upgraded with a smoker box attachment, a heavy, vented metal container that holds wood chips and enables you to smoke foods on the gas grill you already have.

VERTICAL GAS SMOKERS

Vertical gas smokers are less versatile, since they only do one thing, but they do a great job of smoking meats and are easy to use.

DRUM-, BULLET-, OR CONE-SHAPED SMOKERS

Charcoal-fired drum, bullet, and cone- or egg-shaped smokers are more expensive, but they create great smoky flavour and are easy to keep at a low temperature, which is essential if you want smoky flavour without drying out your food.

If you're serious about smoking, pellet smokers — grills fuelled by burning small pellets of compressed hardwood sawdust — are the way to go. They are easy to use, hold a temperature well and create a distinctive, yet still delicate, smoky flavour.

Get Things Cookin'

No matter what type of grill you choose and whether you're using gas, wood or charcoal, barbecuing is a fun and easy way to make tasty meals. Using three main methods — direct-heat cooking, indirect-heat cooking and smoking — you can use your barbecue or grill to make a head-spinning, mouth-watering array of foods.

DIRECT-HEAT COOKING

Direct-heat grilling refers to the intense, high-heat grilling most people use to sear a steak, quick-cook burgers to a beautiful medium-rare, or grill salmon just until it has those nice black grill marks and is cooked through but still moist and tender in the middle. Use direct-heat cooking when you want to sear the food quickly, give it a nice charred flavour and caramelize the outside without drying out the centre. Ideally, foods that you intend to cook over direct heat should be seasoned with dry spices or spice rubs. They can also be marinated, but if you use a glaze that contains sugar, wait until the end of the cooking time to brush it on to prevent the sugar from burning.

The direct-heat grilling method is ideal for steaks, chops, burgers, fish, shellfish, chicken, sausages and vegetables.

In direct cooking, the food is cooked directly above the heat source. With charcoal, this means simply placing the pile of hot coals under the area where you plan to cook. You can even use one side of the grill for direct-heat cooking by pushing all of the coals to that side, but leaving the other side of the grill open for indirect cooking. To use direct-heat cooking on a gas, wood-fired or electric grill, simply place the food directly over the burners or heat source.

No matter how much of the grill you intend to use for direct-heat cooking, it's a good idea to oil the grate to keep your food from sticking. To oil the grate, soak a folded paper towel with oil and then use a grill-cleaning brush or long-handled barbecue tongs to rub the oil-soaked towel over the grate until it is nicely coated with oil. Note that the oil will smoke a bit as you do this, but this is perfectly fine.

Direct-heat cooking, then, is accomplished by placing the food onto the oiled grate directly over very hot coals or hot burners, cooking for a few minutes on one side, then turning and cooking for a few minutes on the other.

INDIRECT-HEAT COOKING

Indirect-heat cooking is a 'low-and-slow' method of barbecuing where you place the food on a hot grill, but not directly on top of the heat source. Additionally, the grill's cover is kept closed during cooking to keep the heat in. When using charcoal or wood, you simply push the hot coals or wood to the side to make a space on the grill that does not have the heat directly under it. On a gas grill, you can accomplish the same thing by heating up the grill with all of the burners on and then turning off one or two of them to make a space where you can cook the food without it being directly over the heat source.

This method is best for longer-cooking cuts of meat, such as roasts, whole chickens or turkeys, and other slow-cooking foods.

As in direct-heat cooking, it's a good idea to oil the grate to keep your food from sticking. Heat the grill first, then move the coals away from your cooking area or cut off the burners in that area, soak a folded paper towel with oil and then use a grill-cleaning brush or long-handled barbecue tongs to rub the oil-soaked towel over the grate until it is nicely coated with oil.

SMOKING

Smoking is a general term for using heat and smoke (from wood and/or charcoal) to cook food. Food is placed onto the grill, which is then closed and filled with heat and smoke (see pages 8 and 9 for smokers and smoker attachments). This process cooks and flavours the meat simultaneously. Smoking is generally done at lower temperatures, which allows the foods time to absorb the smoky flavour while still cooking at a steady enough temperature to safely keep bacteria at bay.

Turn Up the Heat

Here is how to start and heat up various types of barbecue.

COOKING WITH WOOD

To build a wood fire, follow these simple steps.

1. Make a small pile of twigs and paper scraps on the charcoal grate of your barbecue.

2. Over the twig pile, construct a 'teepee' of small sticks, balancing the sticks against each other so that they stand up with room for air to circulate underneath.

3. Light a match and hold it to the twigs and paper scraps until they ignite. Light the sticks in several places.

4. When the sticks catch fire, begin adding increasingly larger pieces, waiting for them to catch fire before adding more.

5. Once you've got a good strong fire, begin adding the larger logs, being sure to lean them against each other, always leaving room for air to circulate underneath.

6. Once the fire is blazing, let it go for about 40 minutes for a really hot heat source. Once the logs are glowing and hot, use a poker, barbecue tongs or a long stick to distribute them as you wish under the grill.

CHARCOAL BRIQUETTES IN A CHIMNEY STARTER

To light charcoal briquettes, a chimney starter — a cylindrical device that allows you to light your briquettes quickly and without lighter fluid — is highly recommended. If you've got one, put it on the charcoal grate of your barbecue, fill the bottom section with wadded-up newspaper and fill the top section with charcoal briquettes. Using a match or lighter, ignite the newspaper. Once the coals catch fire, give them about 20 minutes to get hot. Once all of the briquettes are coated with white ash they are ready to spread out. Carefully tip them out of the chimney onto the charcoal grate and spread the coals out using a long stick or barbecue tongs.

CHARCOAL BRIQUETTES WITH LIGHTER FLUID

If using regular, untreated charcoal briquettes without a chimney starter, make a pile of the briquettes on the charcoal grate of your barbecue. Douse the pile with lighter fluid and give it a few minutes to soak in (while you wait, place the cap securely on the lighter fluid container and place it at a safe distance from the barbecue). Using a match or lighter, light the briquettes in several places and let them burn for 30—40 minutes, until they are all glowing red and covered with white ash. Once they're hot enough, spread them out for an even cooking area using barbecue tongs or a long stick.

EASY-LIGHT BRIQUETTES

Easy-light briquettes are pretreated with lighter fluid, making them convenient and easy to use. Simply pile pretreated briquettes on the charcoal grate of your barbecue and light with a match. The briquettes will be ready for grilling when they are glowing and mostly covered with white ash, which will take about 30—40 minutes. Once they're hot enough, spread them out for an even cooking area using barbecue tongs or a long stick.

LIGHTING A GAS GRILL

The most important thing to remember when lighting a gas grill is to do so with the lid open. Otherwise there is the potential for gas to build up inside. In this case, sudden ignition could lead to a dangerous explosion. Beyond that, every gas grill is a bit different so simply follow the manufacturers' instructions for lighting and preheating.

LOW, MEDIUM AND HOT HEAT

Surely one of the most important elements of a good barbecue is getting the heat just right. If you don't, then no matter how good your recipe or ingredients are, your results could be disastrous. But this simple technique will prevent culinary mishaps caused by a too hot or too cool fire.

To roughly determine how hot a fire is, place your hand just above the grill and count seconds (for example 'one Mississippi, two Mississippi...'). When a fire is hot (hot heat or 230°C—290°C/450°F—550°F), you'll need to pull your hand away in 1—2 seconds. With a medium fire (medium heat or 160°C—180°C /325°F—350°F), you'll be able to keep your hand there for about 3 seconds. With a low fire (low heat or 110°C—120°C/225°F—250°F), you can keep your hand there for 4—5 seconds.

In this book, the recipes state to preheat to certain temperatures. These temperatures are:

Low: 110°C–120°C/225°F–250°F
Medium-low: 130°C–150°C/260°F–300°F
Medium: 160°C–180°C/325°F–350°F
Medium-hot: 190°C–220°C/375°F–425°F
Hot: 230°C–290°C/450°F–550°F

Please check the barbecue temperature is correct using a thermometer before starting to cook for absolute accuracy.

BASIC GEAR YOU NEED

Once you've got your grill and fuel sorted, there are just a few more tools you'll need to invest in. You can find any number of fun barbecue tools that may enhance your barbecue, but here is a list of absolutely essential barbecue tools (for more on barbecue tools, see page 148):

TONGS

A nice sturdy pair of long-handled tongs is essential for manoeuvering hot food around the grill. Stainless steel, spring-loaded tongs are good for durability and ease of use. A second pair of tongs reserved for moving around hot coals and other non-food items is also extremely handy.

SKEWERS

There are really two choices to consider when choosing skewers. The first is disposable bamboo skewers. The benefits of these are that they are inexpensive and don't need to be cleaned. Of course, their disposability can also be seen as a negative. Another downside is that they need to be pre-soaked in water for 30 minutes before placing on a hot grill to prevent them from burning.

The second choice is long metal skewers with a flat-blade design (as opposed to cylindrical metal sticks). The blade design prevents food from turning on the skewer when you attempt to turn the skewers over on the grill. The fact that these are reusable is a benefit, but of course, that means they must be cleaned after each use. Look for metal skewers with heat-resistant handles, otherwise prepare to use oven mitts to avoid burning yourself on the hot metal when you turn the skewers over on the grill.

BASTER

A long-handled, natural fibre brush (stay away from anything that might melt at high heat!) or a mop-style baster is useful for basting meats with marinade as they cook.

WIRE BRUSH

A long-handled wire brush is essential for cleaning the grill.

THERMOMETER

This is very helpful for checking that the barbecue has reached the desired temperature before cooking.

MEAT THERMOMETER

An instant-read meat thermometer is extremely useful for checking the temperature of meat to make sure it is done. This is especially important with large cuts of meat, such as roasts or whole chickens or turkeys.

Is It Done Yet?

Now that you've invested in a handsome grill, outfitted yourself with essential barbecue gear and are ready to get cooking, let's just take a minute to talk about safety. Cooking food until it is properly done is crucial for avoiding food poisoning, but knowing when food reaches this point can be a tricky business. There are a couple of different ways to test meat for doneness.

WHOLE OR JOINTS OF CHICKEN OR TURKEY

To check a whole chicken for doneness, you can insert a skewer into the thickest part of one of the thighs. If it's done, the juices should run clear. Wiggling a drumstick is another method. If the chicken is done, the drumstick will turn easily and feel very loose.

BURGERS, SAUSAGES AND PORK

These should be cooked until the centre is no longer pink and the juices run clear.

FISH

It's relatively easy to tell when fish is cooked through. Simply press on the fish at its thickest point. If it is done, the flesh will flake easily.

PRAWNS

Cook until they are fully opaque and turn pink.

OYSTERS, MUSSELS AND CLAMS

Discard any whose shells are open before cooking. Cook until the shells open fully and discard any whose shells do not open after sufficient cooking.

THERMOMETER METHOD

If you want to be really safe, opt for the more scientific thermometer method. This method is more or less essential when you are cooking large cuts of meat such as roasts, legs of lamb or whole turkeys. Use a digital, instant-read thermometer inserted at the thickest part of the meat (be sure it is not touching bone) and refer to the chart below.

TYPE OF MEAT	RARE	MEDIUM-RARE	MEDIUM	WELL-DONE
BEEF	51°C/125°F	65°C/145°F	70°C/160°F	77°C/170°F (OR HIGHER)
LAMB	51°C/125°F	65°C/145°F	70°C/160°F	77°C/170°F (OR HIGHER)
PORK	N/A	N/A	70°C/160°F	77°C/170°F (OR HIGHER)
CHICKEN AND TURKEY	N/A	N/A	70°C/160°F	77°C/170°F (OR HIGHER)
DUCK	51°C/125°F	65°C/145°F	70°C/160°F	77°C/170°F (OR HIGHER)

Please also check current government guidelines for the latest information on cooking temperatures.

GENERAL FOOD SAFETY

Use common sense and basic food safety rules when it comes to preparing and storing food outside. For instance, you should always wash your hands before handling food, whether you are barbecuing in your garden or cooking in the kitchen.

Bacteria can grow and multiply in any type of food and they thrive at temperatures between 5°C/40°F and 60°C/140°F. Keep food — especially meat, poultry and seafood — in the refrigerator or a cooler (below 5°C/40°F) until ready to prepare for cooking.

Thoroughly thaw frozen meat, poultry, or fish before grilling to ensure even cooking.

Always keep raw meat, fish or poultry apart from cooked foods. If you use utensils or dishes to handle raw meat, wash them thoroughly before using them for cooked food.

SAFE GRILLING

Fire is a dangerous beast and every time you light up your grill, you are welcoming it into your garden. There's no reason your family can't live peacefully with it, but a few precautions are in order.

1.   Have a fire extinguisher nearby and know how to use it.
2.   Don't put your grill or smoker too close to buildings, trees, foliage or other flammable materials. Check the instructions for minimum distances.
3.   Make sure that one person is in charge of watching the grill at all times.
4.   Minimize flare-ups by keeping your grill or smoker clean. Clean grates completely with a wire brush, empty ashes and brush all surfaces clean after every use.
5.   Inspect any grill, especially a gas grill, regularly to make sure there are no blockages or other problems that could cause a dangerous situation.
6.   If using charcoal with lighter fluid, be extremely careful. Never add lighter fluid to burning coals and, of course, keep the container of lighter fluid tightly sealed and far away from the fire.
7.   Keep children a good distance from hot surfaces and any equipment or fuel.

GET GRILLIN'

Once you've got your grill, your tools and your methods sorted, it's time to fire up that bad boy and start cooking. The recipes here are designed to be easy to use, but they never skimp on flavour. So what are you waiting for? Fire up that 'cue, crack a cold one and get cooking!

Chapter 1
RUBS & MARINADES

How to Use Spice Rubs, Marinades and Glazes

Spice rubs, marinades and glazes add complex flavour to your barbecued foods. Each functions slightly differently and their methods of use vary as well.

SPICE RUBS

Dry rubs are mixtures of dried spices and aromatics that are slathered onto meat before cooking. Wet rubs contain oil or other liquid ingredients. While both types permeate the meat with intense flavour, dry rubs do so without adding moisture to the cooking equation, which is critical if you want crisply seared or charred meat.

A good rub combines the four primary flavours: sweet, salty, sour and bitter. Start with the basics — salt and sugar — and from there you can add any combination of aromatics, such as fresh or dried herbs, onions, onion powder, garlic, garlic powder, dried spices, fresh or dried chillies, etc. to create the flavour profile you are looking for.

Spice rubs can be applied to the meat just before cooking or well in advance. The longer the rub sits on the meat, the more deeply its flavour will permeate. Scoring the meat lightly too will help the flavours to penetrate deeply. You'll need about 2 tablespoons of spice rub for each 450 g/1 lb of meat.

MARINADES

Marinating not only adds flavour to meat, but it also tenderizes it. Generally speaking, marinades contain three types of ingredients. Acidic ingredients, such as wine or spirits, vinegar or citrus juice do double duty, both tenderizing and flavouring the meat. Aromatics, like garlic and spices, add intense flavour elements to a dish. Oils or fats serve to keep the flavours in contact with the food so that they penetrate it. A good marinade includes all three of these ingredient types, but you can get creative and mix and match them however you please.

All meat, poultry and fish can benefit from the flavouring effects of a good marinade. Tougher meats, like brisket or pork shoulder get double the benefits in both added flavour and a tenderizing effect. For these meats, a long rest in the marinade is advised — anywhere from 8 hours to as long as 24 hours or even more in some cases. A whole chicken is best marinated for 4–6 hours and chicken pieces for about 2 hours. Fish or shellfish are quite delicate and need only a very short marinating time — 15–30 minutes is usually long enough for the flavours of the marinade to permeate the fish. Too long and a delicate meat will become mushy.

Always marinate in a non-reactive container such as glass, ceramic, plastic, or stainless steel. And whether you are marinating your food for 15 minutes or overnight, cover it well and keep it in the refrigerator.

GLAZES

Glazing is done at the end of cooking. Glazes tend to be thick sauces with a high sugar content, like classic barbecue sauces. If you put a glaze on food early on in the grilling process, the sugar is likely to burn. Instead, save your glaze until just before the food is cooked, then baste it on generously. Continue to cook briefly, just until the glaze is hot and bubbly.

BBQ Spice Rub

☆ MAKES 9 TBSP ☆

PREP: 5 MINS

COOK: NO COOKING

INGREDIENTS

4 tbsp soft dark brown sugar

1 tbsp mustard powder

1 tbsp salt

1 tbsp pepper

2 tsp paprika

1 tsp dried thyme

1 tsp dried oregano

1 tsp cayenne pepper

1 tsp ground allspice

1. Mix all the ingredients together in a small bowl until thoroughly combined.

2. Rub the mixture thoroughly into meat, poultry or fish just before cooking, if short of time, or up to 24 hours before cooking. If leaving for the maximum length of time, exclude the salt from the rub mixture and sprinkle over just before cooking.

3. Put in a shallow dish, cover tightly and chill in the refrigerator until required.

Cajun Blackened Spice Rub

☆ MAKES 4 TBSP ☆

PREP: 5 MINS

COOK: NO COOKING

INGREDIENTS

1 tbsp cracked black peppercorns

2 tsp paprika

2 tsp garlic powder or crushed garlic

2 tsp salt

1 tsp dried thyme

1 tsp dried oregano

1 tsp mustard powder

½ tsp cayenne pepper

1. Mix all the ingredients together in a small bowl until thoroughly combined.

2. Rub the mixture thoroughly into meat, poultry or fish just before cooking, if short of time, or for several hours before cooking.

3. Put in a shallow dish, cover tightly and chill in the refrigerator until required.

Jamaican Jerk Rub

☆ MAKES 5 TBSP ☆

PREP: 5 MINS

COOK: NO COOKING

INGREDIENTS

4 tsp soft dark brown sugar

4 tsp chopped fresh thyme

4 tsp salt

2 tsp ground allspice

1 tsp cayenne pepper or chilli powder

generous pinch of freshly grated nutmeg

pinch of ground cloves

1. Mix all the ingredients together in a small bowl until thoroughly combined.

2. Rub the mixture thoroughly into meat, poultry or fish at least 2 hours, or up to 24 hours, before cooking. If leaving for the maximum length of time, exclude the salt from the rub mixture and sprinkle over just before cooking.

3. Put in a shallow dish, cover tightly and chill in the refrigerator until required.

Texan-style Rub

☆ MAKES 4 TBSP ☆

PREP: 5 MINS

COOK: NO COOKING

INGREDIENTS

1 tbsp ground dried mild chillies

1 tbsp onion powder

1 tbsp mustard powder

1 tbsp salt

1. Mix all the ingredients together in a small bowl until thoroughly combined.

2. Rub the mixture thoroughly into meat, poultry or fish just before cooking, if short of time, or up to 24 hours before cooking. If leaving for the maximum length of time, exclude the salt from the rub mixture and sprinkle over just before cooking.

3. Put in a shallow dish, cover tightly and chill in the refrigerator until required.

Creole Rub

★ MAKES 10 TBSP ★

PREP: 5 MINS

COOK: NO COOKING

INGREDIENTS

2 tbsp pepper

2 tbsp celery salt

2 tbsp paprika

4 tsp garlic powder

4 tsp dried thyme

2 tsp dried oregano

2 tsp ground bay leaves

pinch of chilli powder

1. Mix all the ingredients together in a small bowl until thoroughly combined.

2. Rub the mixture thoroughly into meat, poultry or fish 1–2 hours before cooking.

3. Put in a shallow dish, cover tightly and chill in the refrigerator until required.

Habanero Chilli Rub

★ MAKES 10 TBSP ★

PREP: 5 MINS

COOK: NO COOKING

INGREDIENTS

2 tbsp paprika

1–2 tbsp dried crushed habanero chillies

1 tbsp garlic powder

1 tbsp onion powder

1 tbsp ground cumin

1 tbsp salt

2 tsp pepper

2 tsp soft light brown sugar

1 tsp cayenne pepper

½ tsp freshly grated nutmeg

1. Mix all the ingredients together in a small bowl until thoroughly combined.

2. Rub the mixture thoroughly into the meat, poultry or fish 1–2 hours before cooking.

3. Put in a shallow dish, cover tightly and chill in the refrigerator until required.

Mediterranean Herb Rub

★ MAKES 10 TBSP ★

PREP: 5 MINS

COOK: NO COOKING

INGREDIENTS

finely grated rind of 1 orange

finely grated rind of 1 lemon

3 garlic cloves, crushed

4 tbsp chopped fresh rosemary

2 tbsp chopped fresh sage

1 tbsp chopped fresh thyme

1 tbsp salt

2 tsp pepper

1. Mix all the ingredients together in a small bowl until thoroughly combined.

2. Rub the mixture thoroughly into meat, poultry or fish at least 2 hours, or up to 24 hours, before cooking. If leaving for the maximum length of time, exclude the salt from the rub mixture and sprinkle over just before cooking.

3. Put in a shallow non-metallic dish, cover tightly and chill in the refrigerator until required.

Szechuan Peppercorn Rub

★ MAKES 5 TBSP ★

PREP: 10 MINS

COOK: 5 MINS

INGREDIENTS

2 tbsp Szechuan peppercorns

2 tbsp coriander seeds

1 tsp allspice berries

1 tsp salt

1. Put the peppercorns and coriander seeds in a frying pan and cook over a medium—high heat for 2 minutes, or until fragrant. Tip out and let cool, discarding any peppercorns that have blackened.

2. Put the peppercorns and coriander seeds with the allspice and salt in a food processor and process until crushed to a coarse powder. Don't process for too long, otherwise the mixture will become oily.

3. Rub the mixture thoroughly into meat, poultry or fish at least 2 hours before cooking. Put in a shallow dish, cover tightly and chill in the refrigerator until required.

Sticky Barbecue Marinade

★ MAKES 200 ML/7 FL OZ ★

PREP: 5 MINS

COOK 5 MINS

INGREDIENTS

55 g/2 oz soft light or dark brown sugar

5 tbsp plum jam

2 tbsp tomato purée

2 tbsp white wine vinegar

1 tbsp wholegrain mustard

1. Heat all the ingredients in a saucepan over a low heat, stirring until smooth. Remove from the heat and leave to cool.

2. Meanwhile, score the meat, poultry or fish deeply with a sharp knife. Put the prepared meat, poultry or fish in a non-metallic dish or polythene food bag.

3. Pour the marinade over the prepared meat, poultry or fish and turn to coat.

4. Cover tightly or seal and leave to marinate in the refrigerator, turning occasionally, for at least an hour or preferably, for meat only, overnight before cooking.

Spicy Beer Marinade

★ MAKES 500 ML/18 FL OZ ★

PREP: 5 MINS

NO COOKING

INGREDIENTS

350 ml/12 fl oz beer

100 ml/3½ fl oz soy sauce

1 tbsp Worcestershire sauce

1 tsp hot pepper sauce

1 garlic clove, finely chopped

1 tbsp wholegrain mustard

2 tsp paprika

1 tsp salt

1 tsp pepper

1. Score the meat or game portions deeply with a sharp knife. Put the prepared meat or game in a shallow non-metallic dish or polythene food bag.

2. Mix all the ingredients together in a jug or small bowl until thoroughly combined.

3. Pour the marinade over the prepared meat or game and turn to coat.

4. Cover tightly or seal and leave to marinate in the refrigerator, turning occasionally, for up to 6 hours before cooking.

Satay Marinade

★ MAKES 225 ML/8 FL OZ ★

PREP: 5 MINS

COOK: 5 MINS

INGREDIENTS

4 spring onions, chopped

1 garlic clove, chopped

2 tsp chopped ginger

6 tbsp peanut butter

1 tsp muscovado sugar

1 tsp Thai fish sauce

2 tbsp soy sauce

1 tbsp chilli sauce

1 tsp lemon juice

salt

peanuts, to garnish

1. Score the meat or poultry portions deeply with a sharp knife. Put the prepared meat or poultry in a shallow non-metallic dish or polythene food bag.

2. Put all the ingredients into a food processor. Add 150 ml/5 fl oz water and process to a purée.

3. Transfer to a saucepan, season to taste with salt and heat gently, stirring occasionally. Leave to cool then pour the marinade over the prepared meat or poultry and turn to coat.

4. Cover and leave to marinate in the refrigerator, turning occasionally, for up to 6 hours before cooking. Garnish with peanuts and serve.

Chimichurri Marinade

★ MAKES 200 ML/7 FL OZ ★

PREP: 5 MINS

COOK: NO COOKING

INGREDIENTS

125 ml/4 fl oz white wine vinegar

3 tbsp olive oil

2 jalapeño chillies

2 garlic cloves

1 tsp paprika

1 tsp salt

½ tsp ground bay leaves

1 tbsp chopped coriander

1 tbsp chopped parsley

2 tsp chopped oregano

1. Score the meat or poultry portions deeply with a sharp knife. Put the prepared meat or poultry in a shallow non-metallic dish or polythene food bag.

2. Put all the ingredients, except all the chopped herbs, in a food processor or blender and process until smooth and combined. Stir in the herbs.

3. Pour the marinade over the prepared meat or poultry and turn to coat.

4. Cover tightly or seal and leave to marinate in the refrigerator, turning occasionally, for up to 6 hours before cooking.

Chapter 2
BEEF

Beef Brisket
with Soy & Ginger Rub

★ SERVES 6–8 ★

PREP: 20 MINS
+ MARINATING
+ RESTING

COOK:
10 HOURS

INGREDIENTS

2 kg/4 lb 8 oz beef
brisket

SOY & GINGER RUB

100 g/3½ oz soft brown
sugar

150 ml/5 fl oz light soy
sauce

150 ml/5 fl oz mirin

2 tbsp Korean chilli
bean paste

4 garlic cloves, crushed

55 g/2 oz fresh ginger,
sliced

1 tsp pepper

1 tsp Sichuan
peppercorns

3 star anise

1 cinnamon stick

1. To make the rub, mix all the ingredients together in a large bowl. Add the brisket and stir until the beef is coated thoroughly.

2. Place the brisket in a tight-fitting non-metallic dish and pour over any remaining rub from the bowl.

3. Cover with clingfilm and place in the refrigerator for at least 24 hours to marinate.

4. Remove the brisket from the refrigerator for at least an hour before you want to cook it. This will allow it come back up to room temperature.

5. Prepare the barbecue for smoking and preheat to low.

6. Place the brisket on the barbecue grill, point-side up, and smoke for 10 hours with the lid on, or until the centre of the meat is no longer pink and the juices run clear.

7. Cover the beef in foil and rest in a warm place for 30 minutes before slicing and serving.

WHEN SMOKING MEATS, IT'S ALWAYS GOOD TO PLAN A FEW DAYS AHEAD AS THIS CAN BE A LENGTHY PROCESS.

Cuts of beef

NECK & CLOD
This requires long, slow cooking and is usually used in mince.

CHUCK & BLADE
This requires long, moist cooking. Blade steaks are good for grilling and frying.

FORE RIB
Single rib cutlets are great for grilling, especially prime rib or rib-eye.

THICK RIB
This is also known as top rib and is usually sold boneless or as a steak for braising.

BRISKET
This cut is growing in popularity and tends to be quite fatty. It requires long, slow cooking.

SHIN
This can be sold with or without the bone and requires slow, moist cooking.

THIN RIB
This is usually sold boned and rolled and is good for pot roasting.

SIRLOIN

Tender, juicy joint that is often marbled with fat. This cut produces steaks such as porterhouse, T-bone and fillet.

RUMP

Lean and tender cut of beef that is versatile and can be used in grilling and kebabs.

SILVERSIDE

Very lean, boneless joint that is suitable for roasting.

TOPSIDE

This cut is suitable for roasting and grilling and topside steaks are also available.

THICK FLANK

This is also known as top rump and is sometimes sold as braising steak.

LEG

This requires long and moist cooking and is often sold as stewing steak.

FLANK

This cut can be fatty so is often used for mince but can be thinly sliced and grilled.

Beef Rib Cutlets
with Caper & Anchovy Butter

✯ SERVES 4 ✯

PREP: 30 MINS
+ RESTING

COOK:
20 MINS

INGREDIENTS

4 tbsp olive oil

1 tsp salt

1 tsp pepper

2 beef rib cutlets,
each weighing 800 g/
1 lb 12 oz

CAPER & ANCHOVY BUTTER

5 anchovy fillets,
chopped

200 g/7 oz butter,
softened

2 garlic cloves, crushed

40 g/1½ oz baby capers

small bunch of fresh
parsley, chopped

1 tsp salt

1 tsp pepper

1. Place the oil, salt and pepper in a non-metallic dish large enough to fit the cutlets in. Add the cutlets and turn a few times to coat thoroughly. Set aside.

2. To make the butter, place all of the ingredients into a medium bowl. Beat well with a wooden spoon until well combined.

3. Prepare the barbecue for direct cooking and preheat to medium-hot.

4. Place the cutlets on the barbecue grill and cook for 10 minutes on each side for medium rare, or to your liking. Turn every now and then and brush with the butter until the cutlets are well coated.

5. When the cutlets are cooked, cover with foil and leave in a warm place to rest for 5 minutes. Slice and serve with any remaining butter on the side.

THE CAPER & ANCHOVY BUTTER
ALSO GOES WELL
WITH ANY MEATY FISH, SUCH
AS TUNA, SALMON, SWORDFISH
OR MACKEREL.

T-bone Steak
with Mushroom Butter

☆ SERVES 4 ☆

PREP: 25 MINS
+ CHILLING
+ RESTING

COOK: 25 MINS

INGREDIENTS

2 large red onions,
sliced into 2.5-cm/
1-inch thick circles

olive oil, for brushing

4 T-bone steaks, 2.5-cm/
1-inch thick

salt and pepper

MUSHROOM BUTTER

115 g/4 oz unsalted
butter, softened

1 shallot, diced

25 g/1 oz mushrooms,
such as ceps,
chanterelle, chestnut,
or a mixture, diced

1 tbsp chopped fresh
thyme leaves
or 1 tsp dried thyme

1 tsp salt

½ tsp pepper

1 tbsp red wine

1. To make the mushroom butter, melt 2 tablespoons of the butter in a large, heavy-based frying pan over a medium-high heat. Add the shallot and cook for about 5 minutes, stirring occasionally, until translucent. Add the mushrooms, thyme, salt and pepper and continue to cook for another 5 minutes, stirring occasionally, until the mushrooms are soft and beginning to brown. Add the wine and stir for 30 seconds to deglaze the pan. Set aside to cool for a few minutes.

2. In a food processor, combine the remaining butter with the mushroom mixture. Scoop out onto a square of greaseproof paper, form into a log, wrap and chill for about 30 minutes, or until firm.

3. Prepare the barbecue for direct cooking and preheat to hot. Brush the onions with oil and season the steaks and the onions all over with salt and pepper. Place the steaks and onions on the barbecue grill and cook for about 5 minutes on each side for medium-rare, or until the onions are soft and slightly charred.

4. Remove from the barbecue, top each steak with a few pats of mushroom butter and leave to rest for about 5 minutes. Serve topped with more mushroom butter and a few charred onion rings.

THIS DELICIOUS MELTED
MUSHROOM BUTTER MAKES A
GREAT SAUCE FOR ANY STEAK AT
A BARBECUE.

Chuck Steak
with Black Bean Salsa

☆ SERVES 4 ☆

PREP: 25 mins

COOK: 8 mins

INGREDIENTS

4 tbsp olive oil

1 tsp salt

1 tsp pepper

4 chuck steaks, each weighing 350 g/12 oz

BLACK BEAN SALSA

400 g/14 oz canned black beans, drained

280 g/10 oz canned sweetcorn, drained

1 small red onion, finely chopped

1 small green pepper, chopped

1 tbsp chipotle paste

1 tbsp soft brown sugar

small bunch of fresh coriander, chopped

4 tbsp extra virgin olive oil

2 tbsp sherry vinegar

1 tsp salt

1 tsp pepper

1. To make the salsa, mix together all of the ingredients in a medium bowl. Leave for 10 minutes to infuse then place in the refrigerator.

2. Prepare the barbecue for direct cooking and preheat to hot.

3. Place the oil, salt and pepper in a non-metallic dish large enough to fit the steaks in. Add the steaks and turn a few times to coat thoroughly.

4. Place the steaks on the barbecue grill and cook for 4 minutes on each side for medium-rare, or to your liking.

5. Rest the steaks in a warm place for a couple of minutes before slicing and serving with the salsa.

IF YOU LIKE YOUR STEAK COOKED A LITTLE MORE, TRY USING RIB-EYE INSTEAD OF CHUCK.

Brined & Smoked
Beef Short Ribs

☆ SERVES 4 ☆

PREP: 20 MINS
+ BRINING
+ RESTING

COOK:
6 HOURS

INGREDIENTS

2 x 1 kg/2 lb 4 oz racks beef short ribs, membrane removed (ask your butcher to do this)

4 tbsp soft light brown sugar

2 tbsp old bay seasoning

BRINE

2.5 litres/4½ pints water

500 g/1 lb 2 oz sea salt crystals

250 g/9 oz brown sugar

10 cloves

20 peppercorns

small bunch of fresh thyme

3 cinnamon sticks

3 star anise

2.5 litres/4½ pints iced water

1. To make the brine, place the water, salt, sugar, cloves, peppercorns, thyme, cinnamon sticks and star anise in a large saucepan. Bring to the boil until the salt has dissolved. Turn off the heat and then add the iced water.

2. Place the ribs in a large non-metallic container and pour over the brine. Place a plate on top to keep the ribs submerged. Cover and place in the refrigerator for 24 hours. Remove the ribs from the brine for at least an hour before you want to cook them. This will allow them to come back up to room temperature.

3. Place the ribs on a board and rub in the sugar and old bay.

4. Prepare the barbecue for smoking and preheat to low. Cook, meat-side up, with a lid on for 6 hours, or until the centre of the meat is no longer pink and the juices run clear. Cover with foil and leave to rest for 30 minutes before serving.

BRINING TAKES A WHILE, SO
IT'S A GOOD IDEA TO BRINE MORE
RIBS THAN YOU NEED THEN
FREEZE THEM. THEY WILL KEEP
FOR SEVERAL MONTHS.

Rib-eye Steak
with Ranch Dressing

✪ SERVES 4 ✪

PREP: 20 MINS

COOK: 3 MINS

INGREDIENTS

4 tbsp olive oil

1 tsp salt

1 tsp pepper

4 rib-eye steaks, each
weighing 280 g/10 oz

RANCH DRESSING

1 tbsp mayonnaise

1 tbsp soured cream

1 tbsp buttermilk

1 tbsp cider vinegar

1 tsp Dijon mustard

1 garlic clove, crushed

4 fresh chives, snipped

sprig of fresh parsley,
chopped

sprig of fresh dill,
chopped

½ tsp salt

½ tsp pepper

1. Prepare the barbecue for direct cooking and preheat to hot.

2. Place the olive oil, salt and pepper in a non-metallic dish large enough to fit all of the steaks. Add the steaks, turning them a few times to coat thoroughly.

3. To make the dressing, whisk all of the ingredients together in a small bowl. Set aside.

4. Place the steaks on the barbecue grill and cook for 4 minutes on each side for medium rare, or until cooked to your liking.

5. Rest the steaks for 2 minutes, then serve with the dressing.

ALWAYS MAKE SURE YOUR STEAKS
ARE AT ROOM TEMPERATURE BEFORE
YOU COOK THEM, AS THIS WILL HELP
THEM TO COOK MORE EVENLY.

Rump Steak Fajitas

INGREDIENTS

1 piece of rump steak,
about 675 g/1 lb 8 oz
and 2 cm/¾ inch thick

4 wheat tortillas

2 tomatoes, thinly
sliced

1 avocado, peeled,
stoned and sliced

4 tbsp soured cream

4 spring onions,
thinly sliced

MARINADE

2 tbsp sunflower oil,
plus extra for oiling

finely grated rind of
1 lime

1 tbsp lime juice

2 garlic cloves, crushed

¼ tsp ground coriander

¼ tsp ground cumin

pinch of sugar

1. To make the marinade, put all the marinade ingredients in a dish, mix together and add the steak. Turn to coat thoroughly and marinate for 6—8 hours, turning occasionally.

2. Prepare the barbecue for indirect cooking and preheat to hot. Oil the grill rack.

3. Remove the steak from the marinade and cook on the hottest part of the rack for 2—3 minutes on each side. Move to the cooler part and cook the steak to your liking. Transfer to a board and leave to rest for 5 minutes.

4. Meanwhile, warm the tortillas. Thinly slice the steak and arrange on the tortillas. Add the tomato, avocado, soured cream and spring onions. Fold over and serve immediately.

Porterhouse Steak
in Red Wine Sauce

✩ SERVES 2 ✩

PREP: 25 MINS

COOK: 30 MINS

INGREDIENTS

2 tbsp olive oil

1 tsp salt

1 tsp pepper

2 porterhouse steaks, each weighing 350 g/ 12 oz

RED WINE SAUCE

1 tbsp olive oil

1 tbsp butter

1 red onion, finely chopped

2 garlic cloves, crushed

small bunch of fresh thyme, chopped

200 ml/7 fl oz red wine

1 tbsp flour

1 tsp Dijon mustard

1 tsp tomato purée

200 ml/7 fl oz beef stock

salt and pepper

1. Place the olive oil, salt and pepper in a non-metallic dish large enough to fit both of the steaks. Add the steaks, turning them a few times to coat thoroughly.

2. To make the red wine sauce, heat the olive oil and butter in a medium saucepan over a medium heat. Add the red onion and garlic and cook for 10 minutes, stirring every now and then until translucent and caramelized. Add the thyme and red wine and simmer until reduced by half, then add the flour, mustard and tomato purée. Slowly add the stock, stirring continually to avoid any lumps, then season with salt and pepper. When the sauce has cooked for a couple of minutes, turn off the heat and keep in a warm place.

3. Prepare the barbecue for direct cooking and preheat to hot.

4. Place the steaks on the barbecue grill and cook for 4 minutes on each side for medium rare, or cook to your liking. Leave the steaks to rest for 2 minutes in a warm place then serve with the red wine sauce.

ALWAYS TRY TO BUY AGED BEEF AS IT HAS A MUCH BETTER FLAVOUR AND IS MORE TENDER.

Cheddar-Jalapeño
Beef Burgers

☆ SERVES 4 ☆

PREP: 20 MINS

COOK 10-15 MINS

INGREDIENTS

675 g/1 lb 8 oz lean
fresh beef mince

1 large egg, lightly
beaten

2 spring onions, thinly
sliced

1–2 jalapeño chillies,
deseeded and finely
chopped

2 tbsp finely chopped
fresh coriander

2 tbsp Worcestershire
sauce

½ tsp salt

½ tsp pepper

115 g/4 oz mature
Cheddar cheese, grated

TO SERVE

4 burger buns, halved
and toasted

tomato slices

lettuce

tomato ketchup

1. In a large bowl, combine the beef, egg, spring onions, chillies, coriander, Worcestershire sauce, salt and pepper. Form the mixture into eight equal-sized balls and flatten them into burgers about 1 cm/½ inch thick. Top half of the burgers with grated cheese, leaving a clear border around the edge of each burger.

2. Prepare the barbecue for direct cooking and preheat to medium–hot.

3. Place the remaining four burgers on top of the cheese-topped burgers and press the edges together to enclose the cheese. Flatten again into burgers 1–2 cm/½–¾ inch thick, making sure that the edges are well sealed.

4. Place the burgers on the barbecue grill and cook for about 5–8 minutes on each side, or until the centre of the meat is no longer pink and the juices run clear. Serve on the toasted burger buns with tomato slices, lettuce and tomato ketchup.

THE MOLTEN CHEESE CENTRE
KEEPS THESE FLAVOURSOME
BURGERS NICE AND JUICY.

Brisket Cheesesteak Subs

SERVES 4

PREP: 20 MINS

COOK: 5½ HOURS

INGREDIENTS

1 kg/2 lb 4 oz beef brisket

2 tsp salt

2 tsp pepper

4 sub rolls

4 tbsp mayonnaise

FILLING

2 tbsp oil

2 tbsp butter

2 green peppers, sliced

1 onion, sliced

1 tsp salt

1 tsp pepper

600 g/1 lb 5 oz pizza mozzarella, grated

1. Prepare the barbecue for indirect cooking and preheat to medium-low.

2. Put the beef on a board and gently rub in the salt and pepper.

3. Place the beef point-side up on the barbecue grill and cook for 5 hours with the lid on. Check that the beef is cooked through and the juices run clear. Remove from the barbecue and leave to cool completely.

4. To make the filling, heat the oil and butter in a frying pan and cook the peppers and onion over a medium heat for 10 minutes, or until the vegetables are soft to the touch. Sprinkle with the salt and pepper.

5. Preheat a grill to high. Slice the beef as thinly as possible and divide into four piles on a baking tray. Top each beef pile with the peppers, onions and grated cheese. Grill until all of the cheese has melted.

6. Cut the sub rolls in half lengthways, spread with the mayonnaise and then fill with piles of the beef mixture. Serve immediately.

CAN'T FIND SUB ROLLS?
TRY USING SMALL FRENCH
STICKS OR A LARGE FRENCH
STICK CUT INTO FOUR.

Beef Sausages
with Scorched Tomato Relish

☆ SERVES 4 ☆

PREP: 30 MINS + CHILLING

COOK: 35-40 MINS

INGREDIENTS

SAUSAGES

1 kg/2 lb 2 oz beef chuck, diced and chilled

100 g/3½ oz beef suet

2 tsp fennel seeds

2 tsp dried thyme

small bunch of fresh parsley, chopped

1 tbsp Dijon mustard

2 tsp salt

1 tsp pepper

1 tbsp tomato purée

105 cm/42 inch sausage casing

SCORCHED TOMATO RELISH

4 tbsp olive oil

2 tbsp red wine vinegar

1 tbsp sugar

4 large tomatoes, halved

1 red pepper, halved and stalk removed

1 red onion, quartered

1 large red chilli

4 garlic cloves

handful of fresh parsley

1 tsp salt

1 tsp pepper

1. To make the sausages, mix the diced beef with the suet, fennel seeds, thyme, parsley, mustard, salt, pepper and tomato purée in a large bowl.

2. Using a mincer, mince the beef mixture using the course mincing plate. Refrigerate the minced meat for 30 minutes.

3. Soak the sausage casing according to the package instructions. Thread the casing onto a sausage stuffer and tie off the end. Fill the sausage stuffer with the chilled filling.

4. Hold the casing steady and fill with the filling. When the casing is filled, lay the sausage down in a straight line and prick all the way along with a pin. Turn over and repeat on the other side. Twist and snip into four long sausages.

5. Prepare the barbecue for direct cooking and preheat to medium-hot.

6. To make the relish, mix all the ingredients in a large bowl, then tip into a baking tray. Place on the barbecue grill and cook with the lid on for 25 minutes, or until all the vegetables are slightly charred and softened. Leave to cool slightly.

7. Tip all of the cooled vegetables onto a chopping board and chop with a knife into a rough relish. Place the sausages on the barbecue grill for 6 minutes on each side, or until the centre of the sausage is no longer pink and the juices run clear. Serve the sausages immediately with the relish.

TRY USING HEIRLOOM TOMATOES AND POBLANO CHILLIES FOR A MORE UNUSUAL RELISH.

Chapter 3
PORK & LAMB

Pulled Pork
with Sweet Potato Mash

 ☆ SERVES 6-8 ☆

PREP: 20 MINS + RESTING

COOK: 12¼ HOURS

INGREDIENTS

3 kg/6 lb 8 oz pork shoulder, skin removed and bone in

RUB

1 tbsp paprika

2 tbsp light brown sugar

1 tsp dried thyme

1 tsp dried oregano

2 tsp pepper

1 tsp garlic salt

1 tsp celery salt

1 tsp salt

1 tsp onion powder

CHILLI SAUCE

2 tbsp yellow American-style mustard

2 tbsp cider vinegar

2 tbsp treacle

2 tbsp tomato ketchup

1 tbsp sriracha chilli sauce

SWEET POTATO MASH

1 kg/2 lb 4 oz sweet potatoes, diced

200 g/7 oz salted butter, diced

1 tsp pepper

1. Prepare the barbecue for smoking and preheat to low.

2. Combine all of the rub ingredients together in a small bowl.

3. Place the pork on a chopping board and massage the rub all over the pork.

4. Place the pork on the barbecue grill, making sure the pork is fat-side up. Close the lid and cook for 12 hours, or until a thick dark golden crust has formed. Check that the centre of the meat is no longer pink and that the juices run clear. Cover in foil and leave to rest in a warm place for 30 minutes.

5. Mix together the mustard, vinegar, treacle, ketchup and chilli sauce in a small bowl. Set aside.

6. Boil or steam the sweet potatoes in a large saucepan until soft when pricked with a knife. Drain and mash, then beat in the butter and pepper.

7. Remove any bones from the pork and pull the meat into large chunks. The meat should be very tender, so this should not be hard to do. Put the pork in a large bowl and tip over the chilli sauce. Gently mix, trying not to break the pork up too much.

8. Serve the pork with the sweet potato mash.

IT'S PROBABLY BEST TO COOK
YOUR PORK FROM EARLY IN THE
MORNING TO AVOID HAVING TO
EAT VERY LATE.

Spicy Baby Back Ribs

SERVES 4

PREP: 20 MINS + MARINATING

COOK: 4 HOURS

INGREDIENTS

4 racks baby back pork ribs, each weighing 500 g/1 lb 2 oz

SPICY MARINADE

2 tbsp soft brown sugar

3 tbsp old bay seasoning

1 tbsp Worcestershire sauce

4 tsp salt

APPLE GLAZE

150 ml/5 fl oz apple juice

2 tbsp olive oil

2 tbsp cider vinegar

1. To make the spicy marinade, mix together all the ingredients in a large bowl then add the pork ribs and turn to coat thoroughly.

2. Lay the ribs in a non-metallic dish, adding any remaining marinade from the bowl. Cover the dish with clingfilm and place in the refrigerator for at least 12 hours to marinate.

3. Remove the ribs from the refrigerator for at least an hour before you want to cook them. This will allow them to come back up to room temperature.

4. To make the apple glaze, mix together the apple juice, olive oil and cider vinegar in a small bowl and set aside.

5. Prepare the barbecue for indirect cooking and preheat to medium-low.

6. Cook the ribs on the barbecue grill for 4 hours, with the lid on. Brush the ribs on each side with the apple glaze every 30 minutes.

7. When the ribs are cooked through and the meat is falling off the bone, remove from the barbecue. Check that the centre of the meat is no longer pink and the juices run clear, then serve immediately.

PORK RIBS TEND TO GET STUCK
IN YOUR TEETH SO IT'S ALWAYS
GOOD TO HAVE SOME TOOTHPICKS
TO HAND.

Apple-glazed Pork Chops

 ☆ SERVES 4 ☆

PREP: 20 MINS

 COOK: 20 MINS

INGREDIENTS

4 tbsp olive oil

1 tsp salt

1 tsp pepper

4 pork chops, each
weighing 350 g/12 oz

APPLE GLAZE

3 large cooking apples,
peeled, cored and
chopped

2 tbsp granulated sugar

juice of 1 lemon

150 ml/5 fl oz dry cider

1. In a non-metallic dish wide enough to hold all the pork chops, stir together the oil, salt and pepper. Add the pork chops and turn a few times to coat thoroughly. Set aside.

2. To make the apple glaze, place the apples, sugar, lemon juice and cider in a medium saucepan with a lid on. Cook over a medium heat for 5 minutes, stirring every now and then.

3. When the apples are softened and starting to fall apart, remove from the heat and leave to cool slightly.

4. Prepare the barbecue for direct cooking and preheat to medium-hot.

5. Using a hand-held blender, blend the apple mixture into a smooth glaze.

6. Cook the chops on the barbecue grill for 6 minutes on each side, brushing with the apple glaze as they cook.

7. When the chops are cooked through, or when the centre of the meat is no longer pink and the juices run clear, brush with the glaze one last time and serve immediately.

THIS DISH MAKES A GREAT
ADDITION TO AN INDIAN SUMMER
BARBECUE IN SEPTEMBER WHEN
YOU HAVE SPARE APPLES FROM
THE GARDEN TO USE UP.

BBQ Pork Spare Ribs

SERVES 4

PREP: 30 MINS
+ MARINATING
+ RESTING

COOK:
2–2¼ HOURS

INGREDIENTS

1 rack pork spare ribs,
weighing 1.8–2.25 kg/
4–5 lb

1 onion, quartered

2 bay leaves

2 tsp whole black
peppercorns

1 tsp salt

Classic BBQ Sauce
(see page 166)

1. Place the ribs in a large saucepan (cut the rack in half, if necessary) and cover with cold water. Add the onion, bay leaves, peppercorns and salt and bring to the boil over a high heat. Reduce the heat to low and simmer for 1½–2 hours, testing occasionally during the last 30 minutes of cooking. Remove from the heat once the meat begins to pull apart with little resistance. Drain the ribs, discarding the onion, peppercorns and bay leaves.

2. Coat the ribs with some of the barbecue sauce, then cover and refrigerate for 2–8 hours. Remove from the refrigerator 30 minutes before you are ready to start cooking.

3. Prepare the barbecue for direct cooking and preheat to hot. Baste the ribs with more barbecue sauce. Place on the barbecue grill and cook for 12–15 minutes on each side, turning and basting every 5–10 minutes until the sauce is caramelized and just beginning to blacken in places. Check that the centre of the meat is no longer pink and the juices run clear.

4. Remove from the barbecue and leave to stand for 5 minutes. Cut into individual ribs and serve immediately.

THESE MEATY PORK SPARE RIBS
ARE PERFECT FOR A PARTY AND
ARE FINGER-LICKIN' GOOD!

Maple-Mustard Pork
with Grilled Peaches

☆ SERVES 4 ☆

PREP: 20 MINS + MARINATING

COOK: 1¼ HOURS

INGREDIENTS

1.25–1.3 kg/2 lb 12 oz– 3 lb boneless pork loin

4 small ripe but firm peaches, stoned and halved

MARINADE

125 ml/4 fl oz maple syrup

125 g/4½ oz Dijon mustard

2 garlic cloves, finely chopped

2 tbsp cider vinegar

1 tbsp finely chopped fresh thyme

¾ tsp salt

½ tsp pepper

1. To make the marinade, combine all the ingredients in a large bowl. Add the pork, toss to coat, cover, and marinate in the refrigerator for at least 2 hours or up to 24 hours.

2. Prepare the barbecue for indirect cooking and preheat to medium-hot. Remove the pork from the marinade, reserving the marinade, and place on the hottest part of the barbecue grill. Cook for about 10 minutes on each side, until browned. Move the pork away from the direct heat. Cover and cook, turning every 10 minutes or so, basting with some of the reserved marinade, for a further 45–50 minutes, until the centre of the meat is no longer pink and the juices run clear. Remove the pork from the heat, cover loosely with foil and leave to rest for 10 minutes.

3. Place the remaining marinade in a saucepan over a high heat and bring to the boil. Reduce the heat to medium and simmer for about 8 minutes, or until the marinade thickens to form a sauce.

4. Place the peaches on the barbecue grill over the hottest part of the grill and cook for 2 minutes on each side, or until grill marks appear.

5. Slice the pork into 1-cm/½-inch thick slices and serve immediately, drizzled with the reduced sauce and with the grilled peach halves on the side.

MARINATING THE PORK
IN MAPLE SYRUP AND MUSTARD
OVERNIGHT GIVES THE MEAT
A FANTASTIC FLAVOUR.

Braised Pork Belly
with Apple & Mustard Ketchup

✫ SERVES 4 ✫

PREP: 25 MINS + RESTING

COOK: 2¼ HOURS

INGREDIENTS

small bunch of fresh thyme

1 bulb of fennel, sliced

1 onion, sliced

1.5 kg/3 lb 5 oz pork belly

575 ml/18 fl oz dry cider

300 ml/10 fl oz chicken stock

150 ml/5 fl oz cider vinegar

55 g/2 oz honey

1 tsp salt

1 tsp pepper

APPLE & MUSTARD KETCHUP

juice of 2 lemons

55 g/2 oz sugar

3 cooking apples, peeled, cored and chopped

2 tbsp American-style yellow mustard

1. Prepare the barbecue for indirect cooking and preheat to medium.

2. Place the thyme, fennel and onion in a deep baking tray slightly bigger than the pork. Place the pork belly on top.

3. In a medium bowl, mix together the cider, stock, vinegar and honey.

4. Pour the cider mixture over the pork and then sprinkle over salt and pepper.

5. Place the baking tray on the barbecue grill and cover the barbecue with the lid. Cook for 2 hours, or until the pork meat is soft to the touch and a crackling has formed. Check that the centre of the meat is no longer pink and the juices run clear.

6. Place all of the ketchup ingredients in a medium microwave-proof bowl. Cover with microwaveable clingfilm and cook on high for 4 minutes, or until the apples start to fall apart. Blend the ketchup with a hand blender until smooth and leave to cool down.

7. When the pork is cooked, remove the pork from the barbecue and leave in a warm place to rest for 30 minutes. Strain the juices from the baking tray into a medium saucepan and simmer until the liquid is reduced by half.

8. Serve the pork with the cooking juices poured over the top and the ketchup on the side.

FOR THE ULTIMATE
SANDWICH, JUST CUT THE PORK
INTO SLICES AND ADD
BREAD AND COLESLAW!

Jerk Pork Tenderloin

☆ SERVES 4-6 ☆

PREP: 20 MINS
+ MARINATING
+ RESTING

COOK:
30-35 MINS

INGREDIENTS

2 pork fillets of equal
length, about 1 kg/2 lb
4 oz in total

vegetable oil, for
brushing

salt and pepper

plain boiled rice,
to serve

JERK MARINADE

3 tbsp allspice berries

3 cloves

2-cm/¾-inch piece
cinnamon stick, broken

½ tsp freshly grated
nutmeg

2 large garlic cloves

1-2 fresh red chillies,
deseeded and finely
chopped

large bunch of fresh
chives, about 40 g/
1½ oz, snipped

2 tsp sea salt

2 tbsp malt vinegar

2 tbsp soy sauce

1 tbsp rum

1. To make the marinade, dry-roast the allspice berries in a small frying pan until you smell the aroma. Using a mortar and pestle, grind to a powder with the cloves, cinnamon stick and nutmeg. Tip into a food processor with the remaining marinade ingredients. Process to a thin paste for 2 minutes.

2. Spread the marinade all over the fillets, rubbing it in well. Cover with clingfilm and leave to marinate in the refrigerator for 2 hours.

3. Place the fillets on a board. Brush the two upward-facing surfaces with oil. Place one of the fillets on top of the other, oiled-sides together, to make a sandwich. Tie neatly with string at 4.5-cm/1¾-inch intervals and brush all over with oil. Season with salt and pepper. Cover and leave to stand at room temperature for 30 minutes.

4. Prepare the barbecue for indirect cooking and preheat to hot. Oil the barbecue rack.

5. Place the meat on the hottest part of the barbecue grill and cook for 8 minutes, turning every 2 minutes, until brown on the outside. Move to the cooler part and cover with a lid. Cook for 20-25 minutes, or until the centre of the meat is no longer pink and the juices run clear.

6. Transfer the meat to a board. Cover with foil and leave for 10 minutes. Carve into slices and serve with the juices that have flowed from the meat and the boiled rice.

CARVE THE COOKED PORK
FILLETS INTO DIAGONAL SLICES
THAT ARE 1 CM/½ INCH THICK.

Cuts of pork

LOIN
The best part of the loin is the end nearest the head so try to get this if available. This cut has a great flavour.

BLADE
This is a small cut, but has a beautiful flavour and is very moist. This is good for making crackling.

SPARE RIB (SHOULDER)
This cut has a gorgeous flavour, as the meat from nearer the head of the pig has a sweeter taste. It is moist and succulent.

LEG (HAM)
This is a very lean cut that is usually cured to make ham, but can also be slow roasted. It needs careful cooking to avoid it drying out.

HEAD (CHEEK)
This sweet cut should be cooked slowly to ensure it's really tender.

TROTTER
The trotters can be stewed, braised or slow roasted and are wonderfully succulent.

HOCK
This cut needs to be slow cooked until the meat falls off the bone, but then it's sweet and tender.

BELLY
Pork belly is great for roasting and it is quite fatty, which gives a moist flavour with good crackling.

HAND
The hand is a large cut so a whole joint is good for feeding a group.

Cuts of lamb

SCRAG END
When this is cut into thick slices, this meat is very good for slow cooking.

BEST END
This is the cut with the best flavour and has very lean, tender meat.

MIDDLE NECK
This cut can be stewed or braised until tender.

LOIN
Loin is a moist, flavoursome cut, good for roasting and grilling.

CHUMP
This is a small and boneless cut that is good for grilling.

LEG
This cut is great for roasting, grilling or frying, and it gives plenty of lean and tender meat.

SHOULDER
This cut carries a little fat and it benefits from slow, long roasting. It needs to be boned and is also good when diced and added to stews.

BREAST
This is the most fatty of all the cuts but, when roasted, it produces a very flavoursome, tender joint of meat.

SHANK
This cut needs to be slow cooked or braised, but will then become very tender and fall off the bone.

Pork Belly Sliders
with Kimchi Slaw

MAKES 14

PREP: 20 MINS + COOLING

COOK: 2¼ HOURS

INGREDIENTS

1 kg/2 lb 4 oz pork belly

3 star anise

1 cinnamon stick

5 dried shiitake mushrooms

5 spring onions

200 g/7 oz sugar

100 ml/3½ fl oz light soy sauce

300 ml/10 fl oz rice wine

100 ml/3½ fl oz rice vinegar

14 slider buns (see page 182)

6 tbsp Japanese mayonnaise, for spreading

KIMCHI SLAW

3 tbsp Japanese mayonnaise

½ Chinese cabbage, shredded

200 g/7 oz kimchi, sliced

4 spring onions, sliced

20 g/¾ oz pickled ginger, chopped

1. Preheat the oven to 180°C/350°F/Gas Mark 4.

2. Place the pork belly, star anise, cinnamon stick, mushrooms, spring onions, sugar, soy sauce, rice wine and rice vinegar in a baking dish. Cover with greaseproof paper and foil.

3. Roast in the preheated oven for 2 hours, or until the centre of the meat is no longer pink and the juices run clear. Leave to cool completely in the cooking liquor.

4. To make the slaw, mix together all the ingredients in a medium bowl.

5. Prepare the barbecue for direct cooking and preheat to medium-hot.

6. Slice the pork into 2 cm/¾ inch thick slices. Place the slices on the barbecue grill and cook for 3–4 minutes on each side, or until starting to caramelize.

7. Cut the pork slices into squares. Cut the buns in half, spread with mayonnaise then fill with the pork and slaw.

ANY LEFTOVER PORK BELLY
FROM THIS RECIPE CAN ALSO
BE USED IN STIR-FRIES OR
NOODLE SOUPS.

Chilli Hot Dogs
with Texan Chilli

SERVES 4

PREP: 20 MINS

COOK: 2½ HOURS

INGREDIENTS

TEXAN CHILLI

4 tbsp olive oil

1 onion, diced

1 celery stick, diced

2 garlic cloves, crushed

350 g/12 oz minced beef

1 tbsp flour

1 tbsp paprika

1 tbsp ground cumin

1 tbsp ground coriander

1 tsp dried oregano

1 tsp onion powder

1 tsp chilli powder

1 tsp dried thyme

400 ml/14 fl oz passata

400 ml/14 fl oz beef stock

salt and pepper

HOT DOGS

4 large hot dog sausages

4 hot dog rolls

yellow American-style mustard, to serve

1 onion, chopped

1. To make the chilli, heat the oil in a medium saucepan and sweat the onion, celery and garlic over a low heat. Cook with a lid on for 10 minutes, or until the vegetables are translucent and softened.

2. Turn up the heat a little and add the beef. Cook for another 10 minutes, breaking up the mince with a wooden spoon.

3. Add the flour, paprika, cumin, coriander, oregano, onion powder, chilli powder and thyme, stirring a few times. Slowly add the passata and beef stock. Season with salt and pepper and cook over a low heat with a lid on for 2 hours, or until the meat is tender and the sauce has thickened. Turn off the heat and leave in a warm place.

4. Prepare the barbecue for direct cooking and preheat to medium-hot.

5. Place the hot dogs on the barbecue grill and cook for 10 minutes, turning every now and then. Check that the sausages are cooked through and the centre of the meat is no longer pink.

6. Serve the hot dogs in the rolls, topped with the chilli, mustard and chopped onion.

THIS CHILLI CAN BE MADE
THE DAY BEFORE; IT'S ALSO
GREAT WITH BURGERS FOR A
SLOPPY JOE.

Hot Links
with Pineapple Salsa

☆ SERVES 4 ☆

PREP: 40 MINS + CHILLING

COOK: 12 MINS

INGREDIENTS

HOT LINK SAUSAGES

1 kg/2 lb 4 oz diced pork shoulder, chilled

2 tsp fennel seeds

2 tbsp smoked paprika

2 tsp dried thyme

2 tsp dried oregano

4 garlic cloves, chopped

2 tsp salt

1 tsp pepper

1 tsp chilli flakes

105 cm/42 inch sausage casing

oil, for brushing

PINEAPPLE SALSA

1 ripe pineapple

1 red onion, finely diced

1 tsp chilli flakes

2 tbsp olive oil

1 tbsp soft light brown sugar

juice of 1 lime

1 tsp salt

1 tsp pepper

small bunch of fresh coriander, chopped

1. To make the sausages, mix the pork shoulder with all the other ingredients in a large bowl until the pork is coated thoroughly.

2. Using a mincer, mince the pork and other sausage ingredients using a course mincing plate. Refrigerate the minced meat for 30 minutes.

3. Soak the sausage casing according to the package instructions. Thread the casing onto a sausage stuffer and tie off the end. Fill the sausage stuffer with the chilled filling.

4. Hold the casing steady and fill with the filling. When the casing is filled, lay the sausage down in a straight line and prick all the way along with a pin. Turn over and repeat on the other side. Twist and snip into four long sausages.

5. To make the salsa, cut the top and bottom off the pineapple and stand upright. Cut the skin away, making sure there aren't brown eyes left on the pineapple. Cut into four equal pieces; remove the core then cut into 1-cm/½-inch cubes. Place the pineapple and the rest of the salsa ingredients into a medium bowl and mix well. Leave to stand for a short while.

6. Prepare the barbecue for direct cooking and preheat to medium-hot. Brush the barbecue grill with a little oil and then cook the sausages for 6 minutes on each side, or until the centre of the meat is no longer pink and the juices run clear. Serve immediately with the salsa.

IF YOU DON'T HAVE THE TIME OR EQUIPMENT TO MAKE THE SAUSAGES, THESE SAUSAGES CAN BE BOUGHT READY MADE.

Italian Sausage Subs
with Peppers & Onions

☆ SERVES 4 ☆

PREP: 40 MINS + CHILLING

COOK: 20-25 MINS

INGREDIENTS

ITALIAN SAUSAGES

1 kg/2 lb 4 oz diced pork shoulder, chilled

2 tsp fennel seeds

2 tsp dried sage

2 tsp dried thyme

bunch of chopped parsley

zest of 2 lemons

2 tsp salt

1 tsp pepper

1 tsp chilli flakes

105 cm/42 inch sausage casing

oil, for brushing

FILLING

4 tbsp olive oil

1 red pepper, diced

1 yellow pepper, diced

1 red onion, diced

2 tbsp red wine vinegar

1 tsp salt

1 tsp pepper

4 sub rolls

6 tbsp mayonnaise

handful of rocket

1. To make the sausages, mix the pork shoulder with all the other ingredients in a large bowl until the pork is coated thoroughly.

2. Using a mincer, mince the pork and other sausage ingredients using a course mincing plate. Refrigerate the minced meat for 30 minutes.

3. Soak the sausage casing according to the package instructions. Thread the casing onto a sausage stuffer and tie off the end. Fill the sausage stuffer with the chilled filling.

4. Hold the casing steady and fill with the filling. When the casing is filled, lay the sausage down in a straight line and prick all the way along with a pin. Turn over and repeat on the other side. Twist and snip into four long sausages.

5. To make the filling, heat the oil in a medium frying pan. Add the peppers and onion and cook on a medium heat for 10 minutes, or until the peppers and onions are softened. Add the vinegar, salt and pepper then turn off the heat.

6. Prepare the barbecue for direct cooking and preheat to medium-hot. Lightly brush the barbecue grill with oil and cook the sausages for 6 minutes on each side, or until the centre of the meat is no longer pink and the juices run clear.

7. Cut the sub rolls down the middle, fill each with mayonnaise, one of the sausages and the pepper mixture. Finish with a little rocket and serve.

Pork Meatball Skewers
with Smoked Cheese Sauce

✫ SERVES 4 ✫

PREP: 30 MINS

COOK: 20–25 MINS

INGREDIENTS

450 g/1 lb pork mince

2 tbsp olive oil, plus extra for brushing

2 shallots, finely chopped

100 g/3½ oz panko breadcrumbs

100 ml/3½ fl oz milk

1 tsp fennel seeds

1 tsp dried oregano

1 large egg, beaten

55 g/2 oz grated Parmesan cheese, plus extra to serve

1 tsp salt

1 tsp pepper

4 large gherkins, sliced

SMOKED CHEESE SAUCE

55 g/2 oz butter

40 g/1½ oz flour

600 ml/1 pint whole milk

1 tbsp yellow American-style mustard

150 g/5½ oz smoked cheese, grated

½ tsp salt

½ tsp pepper

1. To make the meatballs, place the pork mince, oil, shallots, breadcrumbs, milk, fennel seeds, oregano, beaten egg, Parmesan, salt and pepper in a large bowl and mix well to combine. Divide the mixture into golf-ball-sized balls. Place the balls on four metal skewers.

2. Prepare the barbecue for direct cooking and preheat to medium-hot.

3. Meanwhile, make the cheese sauce by melting the butter on a low heat in a medium saucepan. Add the flour and cook until a light golden colour.

4. In a small saucepan, bring the milk to the boil and then add it slowly to the butter mixture, stirring continuously with a wooden spoon to avoid any lumps. When all the milk has been added, add the mustard, cheese, salt and pepper. Remove from the heat and set aside in a warm place.

5. Lightly brush the barbecue grill with oil and cook the skewers with the lid on for 10—12 minutes, turning every now and then. When the skewers are cooked through and the juices run clear, remove from the barbecue and serve with the cheese sauce, sliced gherkins and Parmesan.

IF YOU DON'T LIKE SMOKED CHEESE, THIS RECIPE WILL ALSO WORK WITH CHEDDAR OR ANY BLUE CHEESE.

How to Achieve Maximum Flavour

Having a quality grill and knowing how to use it are, of course, key to grilling up a good barbecue, but there's more to it than just knowing how to light a fire or wield a pair of tongs. Here are our best tips for achieving maximum flavour from your grill.

START WITH THE BEST
Always choose the freshest, highest quality meat available. Better still, get to know your neighbourhood butcher and ask him or her to make recommendations based on what's available.

PREP IT RIGHT
Before you even strike the first match, make sure your meat is prepped properly. Trim the excess fat, score the meat so that the flavours penetrate as deeply as possible, marinate the meat or coat it with a seasoning rub, and leave it to rest at room temperature for 30–60 minutes before placing on the hot grill.

SEASON AT THE LAST MINUTE
Even if you marinate your meat in a mixture that contains salt, much of it is lost when you drain off the marinade. Add salt just before you place meat on the grill to ensure that it comes out nicely seasoned. If you are using a spice rub with adequate salt, this is not a concern.

LEAVE IT ALONE
Ideally you want your meat to have a nice seared crust. In order to achieve this, it is imperative that you back off. Place the meat on the grill and let it cook until deep, dark grill marks appear on the underside before you move it or flip it.

GIVE IT A REST
Letting meat rest for several minutes after cooking keeps it moist and juicy. Remove the meat from the grill and set it on a chopping board. Wait anywhere from 5 minutes (for thin steaks or chops) to 15–30 minutes (for a roast or whole chicken) and then slice or carve as desired.

Lamb Chops
with Tomato-mint Jam

PREP: 20 MINS
+ MARINATING

COOK:
1-1¼ HOURS

INGREDIENTS

8 lamb loin chops or 4 lamb shoulder chops, about 2–2.5 cm/¾–1 inch thick

salt and pepper

MARINADE

4 tbsp olive oil

4 tbsp red wine vinegar

2 garlic cloves, finely chopped

TOMATO–MINT JAM

2 tbsp olive oil

1 small onion, diced

450 g/1 lb plum tomatoes, peeled, deseeded and chopped

1–2 jalapeño chillies or bird's-eye chillies, deseeded and finely chopped

100 g/3½ oz sugar

juice of 1 lemon

½ tsp salt

2 tbsp chopped fresh mint leaves, plus extra to garnish

1. To make the marinade, combine the oil, vinegar and garlic in a baking dish or bowl large enough to hold all of the chops. Season the chops to taste with salt and pepper and add them to the marinade, turning to coat. Cover and leave to marinate in the refrigerator for 2–8 hours.

2. To make the jam, heat the oil over a medium-high heat in a large, heavy-based frying pan. Add the onion and cook, stirring, for about 5 minutes, until it begins to soften. Add the tomatoes, chillies, sugar, lemon juice and salt and bring to the boil. Reduce the heat to medium–low and simmer, stirring occasionally, for about 45 minutes, until the tomatoes have broken down and the jam becomes thick. Stir in the mint, remove from the heat and set aside.

3. Prepare the barbecue for direct cooking and preheat to hot. Place the chops on the barbecue grill and cook for about 5–7 minutes on each side. Check that the centre of the meat is no longer pink and the juices run clear.

4. Serve immediately with the tomato-mint jam and garnish with mint leaves.

THE CHILLIES IN THIS JAM
GIVE THE LAMB CHOPS A SPICY
KICK – ADD MORE CHILLIES TO
TURN UP THE HEAT!

Lamb Burgers
with Tzatziki & Feta

★ SERVES 4 ★

PREP: 15 MINS

COOK: 10 MINS

INGREDIENTS

BURGERS

500 g/1 lb 2 oz minced lamb

1 tsp salt

1 tsp pepper

1 tsp cumin seeds

TZATZIKI

4 tbsp Greek yogurt

small bunch of fresh mint, chopped

small bunch of fresh dill, chopped

½ cucumber, sliced

½ tsp salt

½ tsp pepper

PICKLED ONION

1 red onion, sliced

2 tbsp red wine vinegar

½ tsp salt

oil, for brushing

4 burger buns

100 g/3½ oz feta, crumbled

1. To make the burgers, mix the lamb, salt, pepper and cumin seeds together in a medium bowl.

2. Divide the mince mixture into four equal balls then shape into patties.

3. To make the tzatziki, mix all of the ingredients in a small bowl and stir to combine.

4. To make the pickled onion, mix together the onion, vinegar and salt in another small bowl.

5. Prepare the barbecue for direct cooking and preheat to medium-hot.

6. Brush the barbecue grill with a little oil. Cook the burgers for 5 minutes on each side, or until the centre of the meat is no longer pink and the juices run clear.

7. Divide the burgers between the buns and top with the tzatziki, feta and pickled onions. Serve immediately.

THESE LAMB BURGERS MAKE
A GREAT ALTERNATIVE TO
TRADITIONAL BEEF OR CHICKEN
BURGERS.

Lamb Kebabs

INGREDIENTS

LAMB SKEWERS

1 kg/2 lb 4 oz lamb neck
fillets, diced

2 tbsp olive oil

1 tsp paprika

1 tsp dried oregano

1 tsp ground cumin

1 tsp dried thyme

1 tsp salt

1 tsp pepper

4 large flat breads

4 tbsp Greek yogurt

1 large tomato, chopped

1 small red onion,
sliced

100 g/3½ oz red cabbage,
shredded

small bunch of fresh
coriander, chopped

2 lemons, halved

sriracha or other hot
chilli sauce

1. To make the lamb skewers, mix the lamb, oil, paprika, oregano, cumin, thyme, salt and pepper in a medium bowl and stir to coat the lamb thoroughly.

2. Prepare the barbecue for direct cooking and preheat to hot.

3. Thread the lamb onto four metal skewers. Place on the barbecue grill and cook on all four sides for 2 minutes for medium-rare, or to your liking. Check that the centre of the meat is no longer pink and the juices run clear. Leave the lamb to rest for a couple of minutes in a warm place.

4. Place the flat breads on the barbecue grill and cook on both sides until pliable. This should only take a few seconds.

5. Remove the lamb from the skewers. Spread the flat breads with the yogurt and top with lamb pieces, tomato, onion, cabbage and coriander. Squeeze the lemons over the top and drizzle with chilli sauce.

NAAN BREADS ARE A GREAT
ALTERNATIVE TO FLAT BREADS.
THEY WILL NEED JUST
A FEW SECONDS MORE TO
HEAT THROUGH.

Chapter 4
CHICKEN & TURKEY

Sticky Bourbon
Chicken Wings

☆ SERVES 4 ☆

PREP: 20 MINS

COOK: 30 MINS

INGREDIENTS

1 kg/2 lb 4 oz chicken wings, tips removed

oil, for brushing

RUB

1 tbsp paprika

½ tsp ground cumin

1 tsp dried thyme

1 tsp dried oregano

1 tsp salt

1 tsp pepper

BOURBON GLAZE

2 tbsp bourbon

2 tbsp cider vinegar

1 tbsp Worcestershire sauce

2 tbsp treacle

2 tbsp tomato ketchup

2 tbsp chipotle paste

1 tbsp American-style yellow mustard

½ tsp salt

½ tsp pepper

1. To make the rub, combine all of the ingredients together in a large bowl.

2. Cut each chicken wing in half. Add the wing pieces to the bowl containing the rub and turn until coated thoroughly.

3. To make the bourbon glaze, place a medium saucepan over a medium heat. Add the bourbon and flambé. When the flames have gone, add the rest of the glaze ingredients and simmer over a medium heat until the sauce has reduced by half.

4. Prepare the barbecue for direct cooking and preheat to medium-hot.

5. Thread half of the chicken wing pieces onto two metal skewers, creating a raft shape. Repeat with the other half of the wings. Brush the wings with the bourbon glaze.

6. Brush the barbecue grill lightly with oil and cook the wings for 10 minutes on each side, brushing with more glaze as they cook.

7. When the wings are cooked, the meat should come easily away from the bone. Check that the juices run clear when the thickest part of the meat is pierced with a skewer and the centre of the meat is no longer pink. Remove from the skewers and serve.

TRY MAKING A LARGER BATCH OF THE BOURBON GLAZE AS IT WILL KEEP IN THE REFRIGERATOR FOR AT LEAST A MONTH AND CAN BE USED AS A CONDIMENT.

Cuts of chicken

PARSON'S NOSE
This should be removed before cooking a whole chicken as it makes the meat taste bitter.

NECK
Most people discard the chicken's neck but it can be used to make great stock.

WING
This is the boniest part of the chicken and when cooked on a barbecue or grill, they turn crispy and delicious.

WISHBONE
When deboning a chicken, you will need to remove the wishbone by cutting through the meat at the neck cavity and taking out this bone.

WINGTIP
These can be fried or used to make a tasty chicken stock.

THIGH
The thigh is sometimes sold without the bone and skin and is juicy and flavourful. It is dark meat and can contain more fat than the breast.

BREAST
This is a juicy, white meat cut that is versatile and has very little fat. It is great when marinated and chargrilled, and can be sold with or without the skin.

DRUMSTICK
This dark meat cut is great when cooked in a sticky marinade and eaten with your fingers.

Cuts of turkey

WING
Turkey wings are less popular than chicken wings, but they can be roasted or braised to create a crispy, tasty dish.

PARSON'S NOSE
Although some people consider this a delicacy, the parson's nose is usually removed before cooking.

WINGTIP
These are often discarded but can be useful for making stock.

NECK
Most people discard turkey necks but they can be stewed in curries or Caribbean cuisine.

THIGH
The thigh stays more juicy during cooking if you keep the skin on. It has a higher fat content than breast, but has a deeper flavour.

WISHBONE
The wishbone is usually pulled apart by two people to celebrate at Christmas.

DRUMSTICK
The drumstick requires long and slow cooking but then it is tender and falls away from the bone.

BREAST (CROWN)
The turkey crown is the whole bird without the legs and wings. It is great for roasting for people who prefer the taste of just white meat.

Beer Can Chicken

 ☆ SERVES 4 ☆

PREP: 20 MINS
+ MARINATING
+ RESTING

COOK: 1 HOUR

INGREDIENTS

1 medium whole chicken

1 large can of beer

CAYENNE RUB

2 tbsp olive oil

2 tsp sweet smoked paprika

1 tbsp soft brown sugar

1 tsp oregano

1 tsp dried thyme

1 tsp garlic salt

1 tsp onion powder

½ tsp cayenne pepper

½ tsp salt

1 tsp pepper

1. Combine all of the rub ingredients together in a medium bowl, big enough to fit the chicken in. Add the chicken and massage the rub all over the inside and outside of the chicken. Cover and place in the refrigerator for at least a couple of hours.

2. Remove the chicken from the refrigerator for at least an hour before you want to cook it. This will allow it to come back up to room temperature.

3. Prepare the barbecue for indirect cooking and preheat to medium-hot.

4. Open the can of beer, remove half of the contents and then place the can in a beer can chicken roaster (or see tip on right).

5. Place the chicken over the beer can, inserting the can all the way into the cavity.

6. Cook the chicken on the barbecue grill with the lid on for 1 hour, or until the juices run clear when the thickest part of the meat is pierced with a skewer and the centre of the meat is no longer pink.

7. Cover with foil and leave to rest for 15 minutes in a warm place before serving.

IF YOU DON'T HAVE A BEER CAN CHICKEN ROASTER, JUST BE CAREFUL WHEN PLACING ON THE BARBECUE TO AVOID THE CHICKEN FALLING OVER.

Barbecued Chicken
with Lemon Butter

 ☆ SERVES 4–6 ☆

PREP: 20 MINS

 COOK: 30–40 MINS

INGREDIENTS

1 whole chicken, weighing 1.6 kg/3 lb 8 oz

LEMON BUTTER

115 g/4 oz butter, softened

3 garlic cloves, finely chopped

1 tbsp chopped fresh oregano

1 tsp salt

½ tsp pepper

zest and juice of 1 lemon

1. To make the lemon butter, put all the ingredients into a small bowl and mix with a fork until well combined.

2. Prepare the barbecue for direct cooking and preheat to medium-hot.

3. Flatten the chicken by using kitchen shears to cut along both sides of the backbone to remove it. Next, remove the breastbone which runs down the middle of the breast. Trim off any excess skin and fat.

4. Slide your fingers gently under the skin of the breast and legs to separate it from the meat. Spread 2–3 tablespoons of the butter mixture under the skin. Spread about 1 tablespoon over the outside.

5. Place the chicken on the barbecue grill, breast-side up, and cook for 10 minutes. Baste with more of the butter mixture, turn the chicken breast-side down and continue to cook, turning and basting every 10 minutes, for a total cooking time of 30–40 minutes. Check that the juices run clear when the thickest part of the meat is pierced with a skewer and the centre of the meat is no longer pink.

6. Carve and serve immediately.

FLATTENING, OR BUTTERFLYING, A CHICKEN HELPS IT COOK QUICKLY AND EVENLY SO IT DOESN'T DRY OUT DURING COOKING.

BBQ Chicken Wings

☆ SERVES 4 ☆

PREP: 20 MINS
+ MARINATING

COOK
20 MINS

INGREDIENTS

1 kg/2 lb 4 oz chicken
wings, tips removed

oil, for brushing

BBQ MARINADE

1 tbsp paprika

2 tbsp olive oil

2 tbsp tomato ketchup

2 tbsp American-style
yellow mustard

2 tbsp maple syrup

1 tbsp Worcestershire
sauce

1. To make the marinade, mix together all the ingredients in a large bowl. Add the chicken wings and use your hands to mix and coat thoroughly in the marinade.

2. Cover the bowl with clingfilm and place in the refrigerator for at least 2 hours.

3. Remove the chicken wings from the refrigerator for at least an hour before you want to cook them. This will allow them to come back up to room temperature.

4. Prepare the barbecue for direct cooking and preheat to medium-hot.

5. Lightly brush the barbecue grill with oil. Cook the chicken wings for 10 minutes on both sides, or until they are caramelized, slightly charred and the meat comes easily away from the bone. Check that the juices run clear when the thickest part of the meat is pierced with a skewer and the centre of the meat is no longer pink, then serve immediately.

CHICKEN WING TIPS CAN
BE SAVED AND USED TO
MAKE STOCK.

Chicken Thighs
with Caesar Marinade

★ SERVES 4 ★

PREP: 20 MINS
+ MARINATING

COOK:
20 MINS

INGREDIENTS

1 kg/2 lb 4 oz chicken thighs, skin removed

oil, for brushing

CAESAR MARINADE

4 salted anchovies, chopped

2 garlic cloves, crushed

55 g/2 oz finely grated Parmesan cheese

3 tbsp mayonnaise

1 tbsp Worcestershire sauce

small bunch of fresh thyme, chopped

juice and zest of 1 lemon

1 tsp salt

1 tsp pepper

1. To make the marinade, place all of the marinade ingredients into a non-metallic dish big enough to fit the chicken thighs in. Add the chicken, turning a few times to coat thoroughly. Cover with clingfilm and place in the refrigerator for at least 2 hours.

2. Remove the chicken from the refrigerator for at least an hour before you want to cook it. This will allow it to come back up to room temperature.

3. Prepare the barbecue for direct cooking and preheat to medium-hot.

4. Lightly brush the barbecue grill with oil. Place the chicken thighs on the grill and cook the chicken for 10 minutes on both sides. Check the chicken is cooked by seeing that the juices run clear when the thickest part of the meat is pierced with a skewer and the centre of the meat is no longer pink. Slice and serve immediately.

THIS MARINADE HAS ALL THE
FLAVOUR OF A CAESAR SALAD
BUT WITH NONE OF THAT PESKY
LETTUCE!

Chicken Drumsticks
with Satay Glaze

SERVES 4

PREP: 20 MINS + MARINATING

COOK: 25 MINS

INGREDIENTS

1 kg/2 lb 4 oz chicken drumsticks

SOY MARINADE

2 tbsp light soy sauce

2 tbsp soft light brown sugar

1 tsp turmeric

1 tbsp sesame oil

1 tbsp vegetable oil

SATAY GLAZE

150 ml/5 fl oz coconut cream

2 tbsp peanut butter

1 tbsp sriracha chilli sauce

2 tbsp soft light brown sugar

1 tsp fish sauce

1. To make the marinade, place all of the marinade ingredients into a non-metallic dish big enough to fit the chicken in. Add the chicken, turning a few times to coat thoroughly. Cover with clingfilm and place in the refrigerator for at least 2 hours.

2. Remove the chicken from the refrigerator for at least an hour before you want to cook it. This will allow it to come back up to room temperature.

3. To make the satay glaze, place all of the ingredients in a small saucepan and stir with a wooden spoon until well combined. Cook for 5 minutes, or until slightly syrupy.

4. Prepare the barbecue for direct cooking and preheat to medium.

5. Place the chicken on the barbecue grill and cook the drumsticks for 20 minutes, turning every now and then and basting with the satay glaze.

6. Check the chicken is cooked by seeing that the juices run clear when the thickest part of the meat is pierced with a skewer and the centre of the meat is no longer pink. Glaze one last time and serve.

IF YOU HAVE ANY OF THE GLAZE LEFT OVER, IT'S GREAT IN A NOODLE SALAD, WITH PRAWNS, CHICKEN AND BASIL.

Ancho Chilli, Vanilla
& Cola Chicken

✭ SERVES 4 ✭

PREP: 20 MINS
+ MARINATING

COOK:
45 MINS

INGREDIENTS

4 chicken supremes, skin on

PAPRIKA MARINADE

4 tbsp olive oil

1 tsp dried thyme

1 tbsp paprika

1 tbsp soft brown sugar

1 tbsp ground cumin

1 tsp salt

1 tsp pepper

ANCHO CHILLI SAUCE

2 dried ancho chillies, roughly chopped and stalks removed

1 tsp dried oregano

330 ml/10½ fl oz cola

155 g/5½ oz treacle

1 tsp vanilla extract

400 g/14 oz canned plum tomatoes

150 ml/5 fl oz cider vinegar

1. To make the marinade, place all of the marinade ingredients into a non-metallic dish big enough to fit the chicken in. Add the chicken, turning a few times to coat thoroughly. Cover with clingfilm and place in the refrigerator for at least 2 hours.

2. Remove the chicken from the refrigerator for at least an hour before you want to cook it. This will allow it to come back up to room temperature.

3. To make the sauce, place all of the sauce ingredients in a medium saucepan and cook over a low heat for 30 minutes, or until the sauce has reduced by half. Stir every now and then.

4. When the sauce is ready, remove from the heat and leave to cool slightly. Blend thoroughly with a hand blender.

5. Prepare the barbecue for direct cooking and preheat to medium-hot.

6. Place the chicken skin-side down on the barbecue grill for 6 minutes, then turn over and cook for another 6 minutes. Check the chicken is cooked by seeing that the juices run clear when the thickest part of the meat is pierced with a skewer and the centre of the meat is no longer pink. Leave the chicken in a warm place for a couple of minutes before serving with the sauce.

FOR A SUPER SPICY SAUCE,
TRY ADDING A FEW HABANERO
CHILLIES AS WELL.

Buttermilk BBQ Chicken

SERVES 4

PREP: 20 MINS
+ MARINATING
+ RESTING

COOK: 25 MINS

INGREDIENTS

2 small chickens

BUTTERMILK MARINADE

300 ml/10 fl oz buttermilk

2 tbsp olive oil

2 tsp paprika

1 tsp garlic salt

1 tsp celery salt

1 tsp onion powder

1 tsp dried oregano

1 tsp chilli flakes

1 tsp pepper

1. Cut the chickens in half by removing the backbone then cut through the breastbone. Score the chickens on the flesh side as this will help speed up the cooking process.

2. To make the marinade, mix together all the ingredients in a large bowl. Add the chicken halves and mix well until the chicken is well coated. Cover the bowl with clingfilm and leave to marinate in the refrigerator for 2 hours.

3. Remove the chicken halves from the refrigerator for at least an hour before you want to cook them. This will allow them to come back up to room temperature.

4. Prepare the barbecue for direct cooking and preheat to medium-hot.

5. Place the chicken halves skin-side up on the barbecue grill and cook for 15 minutes with a lid on. Turn the chicken over and cook for a further 10 minutes. Ensure chicken is cooked by checking the juices run clear when the thickest part of the meat is pierced with a skewer and the centre of the meat is no longer pink. Leave the chicken to rest in a warm place for 5 minutes before serving.

THIS RECIPE WORKS WELL FOR MAKING SOUTHERN FRIED CHICKEN. JUST COAT IN SEASONED FLOUR AND DEEP FRY FOR 15 MINUTES.

Whole Roast Chicken
with Jerk Spices

SERVES 4

PREP: 20 MINS
+ MARINATING
+ RESTING

COOK: 1 HOUR

INGREDIENTS

1 medium whole chicken

lime wedges and hot
chilli sauce, to serve

JERK MARINADE

2 tsp allspice

1 tsp mixed spice

3 cloves

4 spring onions

1 garlic clove

small bunch of
fresh thyme

1 Scotch bonnet chilli

small bunch of fresh
coriander

2 tbsp cider vinegar

juice of 1 lime

zest and juice of 1
clementine

3 tbsp honey

1 tsp salt

1 tsp pepper

1. To make the marinade, place all of the ingredients in a food processor and blend until smooth. You may need to scrape down the sides of the bowl a few times.

2. Place the chicken in a large bowl and tip the marinade over the chicken. Using your hands, rub the marinade all over the inside and outside of the chicken. Cover with clingfilm and leave in the refrigerator for two hours.

3. Remove the chicken from the refrigerator for at least an hour before you want to cook it. This will allow it to come back up to room temperature. Place the chicken in a deep roasting tray, with a small amount of water in the tray.

4. Prepare the barbecue for indirect cooking and preheat to medium.

5. Place the tray in the centre of the barbecue with the lid on and cook for 1 hour, or until the juices run clear when the thickest part of the chicken is pierced with a skewer and the centre of the meat is no longer pink.

6. Leave the chicken to rest in a warm place for 5 minutes, then serve with lime wedges and chilli sauce.

YOU CAN ALSO TRY THIS
MARINADE WITH A MEATY FISH,
SUCH AS SNAPPER, BASS
OR SALMON.

Honey & Orange
Turkey Breast

SERVES 4

PREP: 30 MINS
+ BRINING
+ RESTING

COOK: 6 HOURS

INGREDIENTS

3 kg/6 lb 8 oz turkey
crown, skin on

BRINE

2.5 litres/4½ pints
water

500 g/1 lb 2 oz sea salt
crystals

250 g/9 oz honey

zest and juice of
3 oranges

10 cloves

20 peppercorns

small bunch of fresh
thyme, chopped

3 cinnamon sticks

2.5 litres/4½ pints
cranberry juice

1. To make the brine, place 575 ml/18 fl oz of the water in a large saucepan. Add the salt, honey, orange zest, orange juice, cloves, peppercorns, thyme and cinnamon sticks. Bring to the boil until the salt has dissolved. Turn off the heat and then add the rest of the water. Add the cranberry juice and leave to cool completely.

2. Place the turkey crown in a large non-metallic container and pour over the brine. Place a plate on top to keep the turkey submerged. Cover and put in the refrigerator overnight.

3. Remove the turkey from the refrigerator for at least an hour before you want to cook it. This will allow it to come back up to room temperature.

4. Prepare the barbecue for smoking and preheat to low.

5. Place the turkey, skin-side up, on the barbecue grill and cook with a lid on for 6 hours. Check the turkey is cooked by seeing that the juices run clear when the thickest part of the meat is pierced with a skewer and the centre of the meat is no longer pink. Cover with foil and leave to rest for 30 minutes in a warm place before slicing and serving.

THIS SMOKED TURKEY TASTES
GREAT ON ITS OWN AND IT ALSO
MAKES AN AWESOME ADDITION TO
A SANDWICH OR SALAD.

Turkey Drumsticks
with Mexican Spice Rub

☆ SERVES 4 ☆

PREP: 20 MINS
+ MARINATING
+ RESTING

COOK:
40 MINS

INGREDIENTS

4 turkey drumsticks,
each weighing 500 g/
1 lb 2 oz

MEXICAN RUB

2 tbsp soft brown sugar

2 tbsp olive oil

zest and juice of
1 orange

1 tbsp salt

1 tbsp paprika

1 tsp pepper

1 tsp garlic salt

1 tbsp chipotle purée

1 tbsp ground cumin

1 tsp dried oregano

1 tsp dried thyme

1. To make the rub, mix all of the ingredients together in a large bowl. Add the turkey drumsticks, turning a few times to coat thoroughly.

2. Cover with clingfilm and place in the refrigerator for at least 2 hours. Remove the drumsticks from the refrigerator for at least an hour before you want to cook them. This will allow them to come back up to room temperature.

3. Prepare the barbecue for indirect cooking and preheat to medium.

4. Place the turkey on the barbecue grill and cook for 40 minutes with the lid on. Check the turkey is cooked by seeing that the juices run clear when the thickest part of the meat is pierced with a skewer and the centre of the meat is no longer pink.

5. Cover with foil and leave to rest in a warm place before serving.

WET RUBS CAN BE MADE WELL IN
ADVANCE AND KEPT IN A JAR IN
THE REFRIGERATOR FOR UP
TO TWO WEEKS.

Teriyaki Chicken Skewers

 SERVES 4

 PREP: 20 MINS + MARINATING   COOK: 20 MINS

INGREDIENTS

500 g/1 lb 2 oz
skinless, boneless
chicken thighs

2 tbsp light soy sauce

1 tbsp sesame oil

1 tbsp vegetable oil,
plus extra for brushing

1 bunch of spring
onions, cut into 5-cm/
2-inch pieces

TERIYAKI SAUCE

2 tbsp light soy sauce

2 tbsp mirin

1 tbsp rice vinegar

2.5-cm/1-inch piece of
fresh ginger, sliced

55 g/2 oz sugar

1. Cut the chicken into bite-sized pieces and place in a non-metallic bowl. Add the soy sauce and the oils and mix until the pieces are coated thoroughly.

2. Cover the bowl with clingfilm and place in the refrigerator for at least 2 hours. Remove the chicken from the refrigerator for at least an hour before you want to cook it. This will allow it to come back up to room temperature.

3. To make the sauce, heat all of the ingredients in a small saucepan over a medium heat until it is reduced by half and slightly syrupy. Remove from the heat and discard the ginger.

4. Prepare the barbecue for direct cooking and preheat to medium-hot.

5. Place the chicken pieces and spring onions onto four metal skewers.

6. Lightly brush the barbecue grill with oil and cook the skewers for 5 minutes on each side. Brush the chicken skewers with the teriyaki sauce while cooking.

7. Check the chicken is cooked and the centre of the meat is no longer pink. Brush the chicken pieces and spring onions with the sauce one last time and serve.

ALWAYS WASH THE SPRING
ONIONS BEFORE USE TO REMOVE
ANY GRIT OR DIRT.

What's Going Wrong?

Five Common BBQ Mistakes and How to Fix Them

A true barbecue master makes grilling look easy, but there are plenty of ways even a barbecue guru can screw it up. Here are the five most common barbecue mistakes and a bit of advice about what to do instead. Read up before the weekend and you'll show them who's boss!

1. Using a dirty grill: There's no nice way to say this. A dirty grill is gross. Your guests don't want to eat the remnants of last weekend's cookout. The solution? Clean your grill every time you use it. You can use a metal brush or a wadded-up piece of aluminium foil to scrape the nasty bits off.

2. Your food tastes like lighter fluid: Lighter fluid is really helpful when you go to light your coals. The problem is that it can often impart a foul taste to the food you've worked so hard to prepare. The solution is surprisingly simple: Skip the lighter fluid. Either use a chimney starter, a cylindrical device that helps get coals going without the need for lighter fluid, or use a gas grill instead of charcoal. Simple as that.

3. Grilling too soon: If you don't adequately preheat the grill, you run the risk of burning food on the outside before it cooks through. Allow a minimum of 10 minutes to heat up a gas grill and 30–40 minutes for a charcoal barbecue.

4. Food is undercooked or takes much longer than you expected: Undercooked food isn't just unpleasant, it can be a real disaster if it makes you or one of your guests sick. The key to cooking food to the proper temperature is to make sure the heat is high enough on your barbecue and, if cooking with the lid closed, don't open the lid more often than necessary. Every time you open the lid, you lose enough heat that you'll need to add a minimum of about 5 more minutes to your total cooking time.

5. Pressing on meat while it cooks: We know it's tempting to press down on meat, especially burgers, while it's cooking so that you can hear the sizzle of the liquid that drips down onto the hot coals. But doing so is a big barbecue no-no. This one is kind of a no-brainer when you think about it: If you want juicy meat or burgers, don't squeeze the juiciness out while they cook. Let the meat sit on the grill without disturbing it until the underside is deeply marked with grill marks. Flip once. Cook until done. You're welcome!

Bacon-wrapped Chicken
Burger with Grilled Pineapple

SERVES 4

PREP: 20 MINS

COOK: 25 MINS

INGREDIENTS

8 smoked pancetta rashers

4 skinless, boneless chicken breasts

oil, for brushing

1 baby gem lettuce, shredded

4 burger buns

GRILLED PINEAPPLE

½ a medium pineapple

1 tbsp demerara sugar

1 tsp pepper

RUSSIAN DRESSING

3 tbsp mayonnaise

1 tbsp tomato ketchup

1 tbsp horseradish

2 tsp hot pepper sauce

1 tbsp Worcestershire sauce

1 shallot, grated

1. Lay two slices of the pancetta rashers next to each other on a chopping board. Place a chicken breast on top of the rashers and wrap the rashers all the way around the breast. Repeat with the other three breasts.

2. To make the grilled pineapple, peel the pineapple and cut into four thick rings. Remove the core then sprinkle each ring on both sides with the sugar and pepper.

3. Prepare the barbecue for direct cooking and preheat to medium-hot.

4. To make the dressing, mix all the ingredients together in a bowl then set aside.

5. Brush your barbecue grill with oil, then place the chicken breasts on the grill. Cook for 10 minutes on each side, or until the juices run clear when the thickest part of the meat is pierced with a skewer and the centre of the meat is no longer pink. When the chicken is cooked, remove from the heat and leave in a warm place to rest for 4 minutes.

6. While you are waiting for the chicken to rest, grill the pineapple rings for 2 minutes on each side, or until caramelized.

7. Divide the chicken, pineapple rings, lettuce and dressing between the burger buns and serve immediately.

THIS BURGER IS A REAL MIX OF GORGEOUS FLAVOURS, WITH THE CHICKEN, BACON, PINEAPPLE AND DRESSING ALL PACKING A PUNCH.

Turkey Skewers
with Avocado Salsa

★ SERVES 4 ★

PREP: 20 MINS + MARINATING

COOK: 5 MINS

INGREDIENTS

4 turkey steaks, 500 g/
1 lb 2 oz in total

olive oil, for brushing

warm tortillas, to serve

MARINADE

juice of 1 orange

juice of 2 limes

2 garlic cloves, crushed

1 tsp paprika

½ tsp salt

½ tsp chilli powder

½ tsp cumin seeds,
crushed

¼ tsp pepper

4 tbsp olive oil

AVOCADO SALSA

2 avocados, finely diced

juice of 1 lime

1 small red onion,
finely diced

1 tbsp chopped fresh
coriander

salt

1. Halve the turkey steaks horizontally to make 8 thinner pieces. Place between two sheets of clingfilm and pound with a meat mallet until flattened to 1 cm/½ inch thick. Slice into strips about 4 cm/1½ inches wide and 6 cm/2½ inches long. Place in a single layer in a shallow dish.

2. To make the marinade, whisk together all the ingredients in a small bowl and pour over the turkey. Cover with clingfilm and leave in the refrigerator to marinate for at least 4 hours or overnight. Remove the turkey from the refrigerator for at least an hour before you want to cook it. This will allow it to come back up to room temperature.

3. Prepare the barbecue for direct cooking and preheat to hot.

4. To make the salsa, carefully mix the ingredients together and leave to stand at room temperature to allow the flavours to develop.

5. Remove the turkey from the marinade and lightly brush with oil. Thread the turkey pieces concertina-style onto metal skewers. Brush the barbecue grill with oil. Grill for 2–2½ minutes on each side, or until the juices run clear when the thickest part of the meat is pierced with a skewer and the centre is no longer pink.

6. Remove the turkey from the skewers and serve immediately with the avocado salsa and tortillas.

THE LIME-INFUSED AVOCADO SALSA IS A GREAT COMPLEMENT TO THE FLAVOUR OF THE TURKEY SKEWERS.

Chapter 5
FISH & SEAFOOD

Whole Grilled Prawns
in Maple & Sriracha Butter

☆ SERVES 4 ☆

PREP: 15 MINS

COOK: 10-15 MINS

INGREDIENTS

1 kg/2 lb 4 oz whole large raw prawns

MAPLE & SRIRACHA BUTTER

150 g/5½ oz butter

2 tbsp maple syrup

2 tbsp sriracha chilli sauce

1 tbsp cider vinegar

½ tsp salt

½ tsp pepper

1. Prepare the barbecue for direct cooking and preheat to hot.

2. Thread half of the prawns onto two metal skewers, creating a raft shape. This will make cooking the prawns a lot easier. Repeat with the other half of the prawns.

3. To make the butter, melt the butter in a small saucepan over a low heat. Add the maple syrup, chilli sauce, vinegar, salt and pepper and stir to combine. Remove from the heat and keep in a warm place.

4. Place the prawns on the barbecue grill and cook for 3 minutes on both sides, or until cooked through and the shells have turned dark pink.

5. Once the prawns are cooked, remove the skewers. Place the prawns in a medium bowl and pour over the butter. Mix well and serve immediately.

IF USING WOODEN SKEWERS, MAKE SURE YOU SOAK THEM FIRST TO STOP THEM BURNING.

Spice-rubbed Salmon
with Coriander Pesto

★ SERVES 4 ★

PREP: 20 MINS

COOK: 8 MINS

INGREDIENTS

1 tbsp cumin seeds

1 tsp coriander seeds

4 salmon steaks, about
175 g/6 oz each, skin on

olive oil, for brushing

salt and pepper

CORIANDER PESTO

2 small garlic cloves

large bunch of fresh
coriander, large stems
discarded

large bunch of fresh
flat-leaf parsley, large
stems discarded

3 spring onions, white
and light green parts
only

1–2 bird's-eye chillies
or jalapeño chillies,
deseeded

125 ml/4 fl oz olive oil

juice of 1 lemon

1 tsp salt

1. To make the pesto, chop the garlic in a food
processor. Add the coriander, parsley, spring
onions and chillies and process until finely
chopped. Add the oil, lemon juice and salt
and process until well combined. Set aside.

2. Prepare the barbecue for direct cooking and
preheat to high.

3. Coarsely grind the cumin seeds and coriander
seeds in an electric spice grinder or in a mortar
with a pestle. Brush the fish on both sides with
oil, season with salt and pepper and coat lightly
with the seed mixture.

4. Place the salmon on the barbecue grill, skin-
side down, and cook with the lid on for about
4 minutes. Turn the salmon over and cook on the
other side for a further 4 minutes, or until the
fish is opaque and flaky when separated with a fork.
Serve immediately, topped with the pesto.

1 **3** **4**

SALMON MAKES A TASTY
ALTERNATIVE TO MEAT AT A
BARBECUE AND THESE SPICES
WORK PERFECTLY WITH
THE FISH.

Scallops
with Hot Soy Sauce

✪ SERVES 2 ✪

PREP: 20 MINS

COOK: 15 MINS

INGREDIENTS

12 large fresh scallops, cleaned and roes removed

1 tsp salt

1 tsp pepper

oil, for brushing

HOT SOY SAUCE

1 tbsp oil

1 tbsp sesame oil

1 garlic clove, chopped

2 tbsp rice wine

2 tbsp light soy sauce

1 tbsp sugar

1 tbsp oyster sauce

2.5-cm/1-inch piece of fresh ginger, cut into matchsticks

4 spring onions, sliced

1 red bird's eye chilli, sliced

1. To make the soy sauce, heat the oils in a small saucepan over a medium heat. Add the garlic and cook for 30 seconds, then add the rice wine, soy sauce, sugar and oyster sauce. Reduce by half then add the ginger, spring onions and chilli. Remove from the heat and set aside.

2. Prepare the barbecue for direct cooking and preheat to hot.

3. Thread the scallops onto four metal skewers and sprinkle the skewers with the salt and pepper.

4. Brush the barbecue grill with a little oil. Cook the scallops for 30 seconds on each side, or until the scallops are caramelized on the outside, but still creamy in the middle.

5. Remove from the skewers and serve with the hot soy sauce.

WHENEVER POSSIBLE, BUY
HAND-DIVED SCALLOPS AS THIS
METHOD HAS MUCH LESS OF AN
ENVIRONMENTAL IMPACT.

Grilled Trout Tacos

SERVES 2

PREP: 20 MINS

COOK: 12 MINS

INGREDIENTS

1 small red onion,
sliced into rings

1 red jalapeño chilli,
sliced

2 tbsp red wine vinegar

½ tsp salt

2 whole trout, gutted
and cleaned, each
weighing 375 g—400 g/
13 oz—14 oz

2 tbsp olive oil

1 tsp dried oregano

1 tsp cumin seeds

1 tsp paprika

½ tsp salt

½ tsp pepper

6 soft tacos or small
tortillas

FILLINGS

1 ripe avocado, chopped

juice of ½ lime

2 tbsp soured cream

55 g/2 oz salted
ricotta, grated

small bunch of fresh
coriander, finely chopped

lime wedges, to serve

1. Place the onion, chilli, vinegar and salt in a small bowl. Mix together with a spoon and then leave to pickle slightly.

2. Score the trout on both sides; this will help speed up the cooking process.

3. In a shallow non-metallic dish large enough to hold the trout, mix together the oil, oregano, cumin seeds, paprika, salt and pepper. Then add the trout, turning a couple of times to coat thoroughly.

4. Start to prepare the fillings by placing the avocado in a small bowl. Squeeze over the lime juice and set aside.

5. Prepare the barbecue for direct cooking and preheat to medium-hot.

6. Place the trout on the barbecue grill and cook for 5 minutes on both sides, or until the flesh comes easily away from the bone. Check that the fish is opaque and flaky when separated with a fork.

7. Leave the trout to cool slightly, and then remove the flesh from the bone.

8. Heat the tacos for a few seconds on each side, until they become pliable. Divide the tacos between two plates then top with the trout, soured cream, avocado, salted ricotta, and pickled onion mixture. Sprinkle each taco with the coriander and then serve with the lime wedges.

GRILLED SALMON OR SEA BASS
WILL ALSO WORK WELL WITH
THIS RECIPE; YOU MAY NEED
TO ADJUST THE COOKING
TIMES SLIGHTLY.

Peppered Tuna Steaks
with Anchovy Mayo

INGREDIENTS

4 tbsp olive oil

1 tsp salt

1 tsp pepper

4 tuna steaks, each weighing 250 g/9 oz

lemon wedges, to serve

ANCHOVY MAYO

1 egg yolk

splash of water

4 anchovy fillets

1 garlic clove, crushed

2 tsp Dijon mustard

200 ml/7 fl oz rapeseed oil

1 tbsp white wine vinegar

salt and pepper

1. To make the mayo, place the egg yolk, water, anchovy fillets, garlic and Dijon mustard in a food processor and blitz for 30 seconds, or until everything has doubled in volume. With the motor still running, start to add the oil very slowly. When all of the oil has been added and the mayonnaise has thickened, season with salt and pepper and then add the vinegar. Transfer the mayo to a small bowl.

2. Prepare the barbecue for direct cooking and preheat to hot.

3. Place the olive oil, salt and pepper in a non-metallic dish large enough to hold all of the tuna steaks. Add the tuna, turning a few times to coat thoroughly.

4. Place the tuna on the barbecue grill and cook for 1 minute on each side for rare, or to your liking. Serve with the mayo and lemon wedges.

HOME-MADE MAYONNAISE IS
AMAZING BUT, IF YOU REALLY
DON'T HAVE THE TIME, SHOP
BOUGHT WILL DO JUST FINE.

Squid
with Burnt Corn Salsa

SERVES 4

PREP: 15 MINS
+ MARINATING

COOK: 12 MINS

INGREDIENTS

4 large squid, each weighing 250 g/9 oz, cleaned and gutted

SPICY MARINADE

4 tbsp olive oil

1 tsp salt

1 tsp pepper

1 tbsp paprika

1 tbsp cumin

juice of 1 lemon

½ red onion, chopped

1 green jalapeño chilli, chopped

small bunch of fresh coriander, chopped

BURNT CORN SALSA

2 corn on the cobs

1 large tomato, chopped

1 small red onion, finely chopped

small bunch of fresh coriander, chopped

1 tsp chilli flakes

2 tbsp extra virgin olive oil

1 tbsp red wine vinegar

1 tsp salt

1 tsp pepper

1. To make the marinade for the squid, mix together all of the ingredients in a large non-metallic bowl large enough to hold the squid. Add the squid and turn to coat thoroughly. Leave to marinate for 20 minutes.

2. Prepare the barbecue for direct cooking and preheat to hot.

3. To make the salsa, place the corn on the barbecue grill and cook until the corn is fairly charred all over. Remove and leave to cool. Leave the barbecue on.

4. Cut the kernels from the corn. Place the kernels in a medium bowl with all of the other salsa ingredients and mix well. Leave to infuse while you cook the squid.

5. Place the squid (and tentacles if there are any) on the barbecue grill and cook for 3 minutes on each side, or until the squid is nicely charred and has formed a cylindrical shape.

6. Slice the squid into rings and serve with the salsa.

TRY NOT TO OVERCOOK YOUR
SQUID AS THIS WILL MAKE IT
VERY CHEWY.

Grilled Lobster
with Nam Jim Sauce

 ☆ SERVES 2 ☆

PREP: 25 MINS + FREEZING

COOK: 20 MINS

INGREDIENTS

2 whole live lobsters, each weighing 675 g/1 lb 8 oz

55 g/2 oz salted butter, melted

1 tsp pepper

NAM JIM SAUCE

small bunch of fresh coriander

10 green bird's eye chillies

½ tsp salt

55 g/2 oz palm sugar

juice of 4 limes

1. Place the lobsters in the freezer for 2 hours before cooking. Bring a large saucepan of salted water to the boil and add the lobsters. Blanch for 5 minutes, then remove and place in iced water for 10 minutes.

2. Cut the lobsters in half lengthways and remove the stomach sack at the head of the lobster. If there is one, remove the black line from the tail of the lobster and any roe in the head area. Crack the claws; this will allow heat in when cooking.

3. Prepare the barbecue for direct cooking and preheat to medium-hot.

4. To make the nam jim sauce, place the coriander, chillies and salt in a food processor. Blend for 30 seconds, then scrape down the sides with a spatula to avoid any lumps. With the motor running, add the palm sugar and lime juice and blend until smooth. Place the sauce in a small bowl.

5. Brush the flesh side of the lobsters with the melted butter and sprinkle with pepper. Place the lobsters, flesh-side down, on the barbecue grill and cook for 5 minutes. Turn over and cook for another 5 minutes, brushing with butter again. When the lobsters are cooked through, serve with the nam jim sauce.

BLANCHING THE LOBSTERS WILL
PREVENT ANY NASTY SURPRISES
OF UNCOOKED CLAW MEAT ONCE YOU
HAVE BARBECUED THEM.

Clams with Smoked Bacon

 SERVES 2

 PREP: 15 MINS + SOAKING **COOK: 15 MINS**

INGREDIENTS

1 kg/2 lb 4 oz fresh clams, scrubbed

SMOKED BACON BUTTER

200 g/7 oz butter

2 shallots, finely diced

2 garlic cloves, finely chopped

100 g/3½ oz smoked bacon lardons

juice of 1 lemon

small bunch of fresh flat-leaf parsley, chopped

1. Soak the clams in fresh water for at least an hour before cooking, then remove from the water and drain well. Discard any clams with broken shells and any that refuse to close when tapped.

2. Prepare the barbecue for direct cooking and preheat to hot.

3. Melt the butter in a large frying pan over a medium heat. Add the shallots, garlic and smoked bacon and cook for 8–10 minutes, or until browned. Remove from the heat and add the lemon and parsley. Set aside in a warm place.

4. Place the clams on the barbecue grill and cook for 4–5 minutes, or until the clams have fully opened. Discard any clams that have not opened at this point.

5. Mix the cooked clams in the bacon butter and serve immediately.

FOR THOSE OF YOU WHO LIKE THINGS A LITTLE SPICIER, TRY ADDING A TABLESPOON OF CURRY POWDER TO THE BACON BUTTER.

Prawn Skewers
with Barbecue Sauce

✮ SERVES 4 ✮

PREP: 15 MINS
+ MARINATING

COOK:
10 MINS

INGREDIENTS

675 g/1 lb 8 oz raw
prawns, peeled and
deveined

2 tbsp olive oil

juice of 1 lime

1 garlic clove, finely
chopped

1 tsp salt

¼–½ tsp ground chipotle
or smoked paprika

Classic BBQ Sauce
(see page 166), for
brushing, plus extra
to serve

lime halves, to serve

1. Place the prawns in a large bowl and drizzle over the oil and lime juice. Add the garlic, salt and ground chipotle and stir to coat well. Cover and chill in the refrigerator for 15 minutes.

2. Prepare the barbecue for direct cooking and preheat to hot.

3. Remove the prawns from the marinade, discarding the marinade, and thread onto metal skewers (three to five prawns per skewer, depending on the size of the prawns).

4. Brush the prawns on both sides with a little barbecue sauce, place on the barbecue grill and cook for about 5 minutes on each side, brushing with a bit more of the sauce from time to time, or until the prawns have cooked through, have turned pink and are slightly charred around the edges. Serve immediately with lime halves and barbecue sauce for dipping.

PLUMP, JUICY PRAWNS ARE
A PERFECT PARTNER FOR
THE CLASSIC SWEET-SPICY
BARBECUE SAUCE.

Chapter 6
VEGETABLES

Cheddar & Dill Pickle
Stuffed Jackets

☆ SERVES 4 ☆

PREP: 20 MINS

COOK:
1 HOUR 10 MINS

INGREDIENTS

4 jacket potatoes

4 tbsp olive oil

1 tsp salt

CHEDDAR & PICKLE FILLING

2 tbsp soured cream

1 small red onion, chopped

100 g/3½ oz strong Cheddar cheese, grated

55 g/2 oz dill pickles, or gherkins, chopped

½ tsp salt

1 tsp pepper

1. Prepare the barbecue for indirect cooking and preheat to medium.

2. Place the jacket potatoes on a baking tray. Drizzle with the oil and sprinkle over the salt.

3. Place on the barbecue grill with the lid on for an hour, or until the jacket is soft to the touch. Remove from the barbecue and leave to cool slightly.

4. Cut the jackets into halves and scoop out the flesh. Place the flesh in a bowl and mash lightly. Now add the filling ingredients and mix well with a wooden spoon.

5. Divide the mixture between the jacket skins and then put back in the baking tray. Place on the barbecue grill and cook with the lid on for 10 minutes, or until lightly golden and bubbling. Serve immediately.

TRY EXPERIMENTING WITH
DIFFERENT CHEESES, SUCH
AS GORGONZOLA.

Seven Totally Unnecessary Barbecue Tools You Won't Want to Be Without

1. Steam-Powered Grill Cleaning Tool
Fill this fancy-looking grill brush with water and the heat from the grill turns it into steam that powers grit and grime off your grate. There are several models available that include ergonomic handles, powerful stainless steel bristles and built-in scrapers.

2. Burger Press
This handy gadget makes it easy to turn out perfectly consistent burger patties. Many models are adjustable, letting you set them for quarter pounder or half-pound burgers. They even add that all-important dimple that keeps it from shrinking up too much and bulging in the centre.

3. Himalayan Salt Plate
A slab of pink salt from the Himalayas can be heated on a grill and used to cook seafood or meat. The salt retains heat and cooks evenly — and it adds complex flavour to the food at the same time.

4. Turner Tongs
Shaped liked spatulas and assembled like tongs, this tool helps you flip foods on the grill with ease. They are especially useful for delicate foods like fish.

5. Vegetable Grill Clips
Vegetable grill clips provide an easy way to grill veggies. Designed like a giant stainless-steel clothes peg, they grip veggie sticks and slices so that you can turn them easily on the grill. Most versions come in sets of four, making it easy to cook individual portions.

6. Wireless Food Thermometer
A wireless thermometer is the ultimate grilling gadget letting you keep tabs on your food while also attending to your guests. Simple versions include a probe that goes into the meat and sends a signal to a receiver, or even your phone, computer, or tablet via Bluetooth, to let you know when the meat reaches your desired temperature.

7. Barbecue Toolbelt
Now that you're all kitted out with cool barbecue gadgets, where are you going to keep them all? A barbecue toolbelt, of course. Designed to mimic the traditional carpenter's toolbelt, these handy wearable organizers provide places to store everything from your turner tongs to your wireless thermometer receiver. And you'll look super cool with it on, too!

Satay Tofu Salad

✪ SERVES 4 ✪

PREP: 20 MINS + MARINATING

COOK: 20 MINS

INGREDIENTS

800 g/1 lb 12 oz extra-firm tofu

MARINADE

2 tbsp soy sauce

2 tbsp sesame oil

2 tbsp mirin (rice wine), sake, sherry or white wine

SATAY SAUCE

80 g/2¾ oz smooth peanut butter

125 ml/4 fl oz coconut milk

2 tbsp soy sauce

2 tbsp soft light brown sugar

2 tbsp hot water, plus extra if needed

juice of 1 lime

2 tsp chilli paste, plus extra to taste

1 garlic clove, finely ground

1 tbsp grated fresh ginger

TO SERVE

lettuce leaves

red and orange pepper strips

cucumber strips

whole basil leaves

---

1. Slice the tofu into 2.5-cm/1-inch thick slabs and pat very dry with kitchen paper, pressing to release the excess moisture.

2. To make the marinade, combine the soy sauce, oil and mirin in a large bowl. Add the tofu and turn to coat. Marinate for at least 30 minutes and up to 8 hours (refrigerate if marinating for longer than 30 minutes).

3. To make the satay sauce, combine the peanut butter, coconut milk, soy sauce, sugar, water, lime juice, chilli paste, garlic and ginger in a bowl and stir to mix well. Add more water, a teaspoon or two at a time, if needed to reach the desired consistency.

4. Prepare the barbecue for direct cooking and preheat to medium-hot. Baste the tofu with some satay sauce, place on the barbecue grill and cook for about 10 minutes on each side, or until golden brown. Cut into strips.

5. Serve the tofu on a bed of lettuce leaves, with the pepper and cucumber strips and basil leaves. Serve immediately with extra satay sauce for drizzling.

THIS TOFU SALAD IS A GREAT
ADDITION TO THE BARBECUE FOR
ANY VEGETARIAN GUESTS OR FOR
ANYONE ON A DIET.

Grilled Stuffed Peppers

 SERVES 4

 PREP: 20 MINS

COOK: 35-40 MINS

INGREDIENTS

4 large red peppers

FILLING

2 tbsp olive oil

1 small onion, diced

2 courgettes, diced

1 tsp salt

1 tsp ground cumin

425 g/15 oz canned chickpeas, drained and rinsed

200 g/7 oz freshly cooked brown rice

zest and juice of 1 lemon

2 tbsp finely chopped fresh mint

115 g/4 oz feta cheese, crumbled

1. Prepare the barbecue for indirect cooking and preheat to medium.

2. To make the filling, heat the oil in a heavy-based frying pan over a medium-high heat. Add the onion, courgettes and salt and cook for about 5 minutes, stirring occasionally, until the onion is translucent and the courgettes are beginning to brown. Stir in the cumin and chickpeas and cook, stirring, for a further 1 minute. Remove from the heat and leave to cool for a few minutes.

3. Combine the courgette and chickpea mixture in a large bowl with the rice, lemon zest and juice, mint and cheese. Stir to mix well.

4. Carefully slice off the tops of the red peppers, then core and deseed them. Stuff them with the rice mixture, then replace the tops and secure them with cocktail sticks or skewers.

5. Place the peppers on the barbecue grill on their sides and cook, covered, for about 25—30 minutes, turning every 5 minutes, until soft and just beginning to char. Serve immediately.

THIS TASTY DISH WILL DELIGHT
BOTH MEAT EATERS AND
VEGETARIANS ALIKE.

Portobello Mushrooms

PREP: 15 MINS

COOK: 5 MINS

INGREDIENTS

1 kg/2 lb 4 oz
Portobello mushrooms

5 tbsp olive oil

1 tsp salt

1 tsp pepper

4 garlic cloves, chopped

small bunch of fresh
parsley, chopped

500 g/1 lb 2 oz
Gorgonzola, sliced

1. Prepare the barbecue for direct cooking and preheat to hot.

2. Remove and discard the stems from the mushrooms. Drizzle the mushrooms with the olive oil, then sprinkle with the salt and pepper.

3. Add the garlic and parsley, and top the mushrooms with the Gorgonzola slices.

4. Place on the barbecue grill and cook, cheese-side up, with the lid on for 5 minutes, or until the mushrooms are cooked and the cheese has melted.

THESE CAN BE MADE IN
ADVANCE AND KEPT IN THE
FRIDGE FOR UP TO A DAY.

Grilled Cajun Vegetables
with Parmesan Grits

★ SERVES 4 ★

PREP: 20 MINS

COOK: 30 MINS

INGREDIENTS

4 tbsp olive oil

1 tsp salt

1 tbsp Cajun spice

2 courgettes, halved lengthways

1 aubergine, quartered lengthways

100 g/3½ oz baby corn

1 red pepper, sliced

1 yellow pepper, sliced

20 g/¾ oz Parmesan cheese, grated

GRITS

1 litre/1¾ pints whole milk

55 g/2 oz butter

350 g/12 oz coarse cornmeal

100 g/3½ oz Parmesan cheese, grated

1 tsp salt

1 tsp pepper

1. To make the grits, place the milk and butter in a medium, heavy-based stainless steel saucepan and warm over a medium heat. When the milk and butter have started to boil, whisk in all the cornmeal. Turn down the heat and stir with a wooden spoon for 10 minutes, or until the cornmeal resembles a light mash consistency. Remove from the heat, beat in the Parmesan and sprinkle with the salt and pepper. Cover and leave in a warm place.

2. Prepare the barbecue for direct cooking and preheat to medium-hot.

3. In a large bowl, mix together the oil, salt and Cajun spice. Add the courgettes, aubergine, baby corn and peppers and mix well to coat thoroughly.

4. Cook the vegetables on the barbecue grill for 4 minutes on each side, or until they are slightly charred but soft to the touch. Serve the vegetables over the grits. Sprinkle with the Parmesan and serve immediately.

TRY USING GRITS AS AN
ALTERATIVE TO MASH – IT'S
GREAT WITH BUTTER, CREAM,
CHEESE AND HERBS.

Baked Sweet Potatoes
with Salsa

SERVES 4

PREP: 20 MINS

COOK: 1 HOUR

INGREDIENTS

4 sweet potatoes,
about 350 g/12 oz each

1 tbsp olive oil,
for rubbing

large knob of butter

2 tbsp chopped fresh
coriander

100 g/3½ oz grated feta
cheese or other salty
white cheese

salt and pepper

SALSA

3 tomatoes, deseeded and
finely diced

1 small red onion,
finely diced

½–1 small green chilli,
deseeded and finely diced

3 tbsp chopped fresh
coriander

juice of 1 lime

1. Prepare the barbecue for indirect cooking and preheat to medium. Use some kitchen paper to rub the potatoes with a little olive oil and sprinkle with salt to coat lightly.

2. Tightly wrap the potatoes in pieces of double-thickness aluminium foil and place on the barbecue grill for about 1 hour.

3. Meanwhile, combine the salsa ingredients in a bowl. Add a little salt to taste. Leave to stand at room temperature to let the flavours develop.

4. When the potatoes are cooked, cut them open, fork the flesh and mix in a little butter, salt and pepper, and most of the coriander. Sprinkle with the cheese and the remaining coriander. Serve immediately with the salsa spooned over the top.

SWEET POTATOES MAKE A
TASTY ALTERNATIVE TO NORMAL
JACKET POTATOES AND CONTAIN
LESS CARBS.

Mediterranean
Grilled Aubergines

☆ SERVES 4 ☆

PREP: 15 MINS

COOK: 15 MINS

INGREDIENTS

GRILLED AUBERGINES

2 large aubergines

4 tbsp olive oil

1 tsp salt

1 tsp pepper

TAHINI YOGURT

2 tbsp Greek yogurt

1 tbsp tahini

1 garlic clove, crushed

juice of 1 lemon

salt and pepper,
to taste

30 g/1 oz butter

100 g/3½ oz pine nuts

handful of rocket

100 g/3½ oz raisins

2 tbsp extra virgin
olive oil, for drizzling

1. Cut the aubergines in half lengthways, then score the flesh on a slight angle into diamond shapes.

2. Drizzle the aubergines with the olive oil and sprinkle with the salt and pepper.

3. Prepare the barbecue for direct cooking and preheat to medium-hot.

4. To make the yogurt, mix together the yogurt, tahini, garlic and lemon juice in a small bowl. Season with salt and pepper.

5. Lay the aubergines on the barbecue grill, skin-side down, and cook for 7 minutes, or until the flesh is golden and soft to the touch. Turn over and cook for another 7 minutes.

6. Meanwhile, heat the butter in a small frying pan over a medium heat. Add the pine nuts and toast until they are a light golden colour. When the aubergines are cooked, divide between four plates and serve with the tahini yogurt, rocket, pine nuts and raisins. Drizzle with extra virgin olive oil and serve.

WHEN USING SALAD LEAVES,
ALWAYS GIVE THEM A GOOD
SOAK IN WATER TO CLEAN AND
REVITALIZE THE LEAVES.

Squash & Polenta
Burgers

✫ SERVES 4-6 ✫

PREP: 25 MINS
+ CHILLING

COOK:
45-50 MINS

INGREDIENTS

450 g/1 lb butternut squash (225 g/8 oz after peeling and deseeding), cut into chunks

150 ml/5 fl oz water

85 g/3 oz instant polenta

115 g/4 oz celeriac, grated

6 spring onions, finely chopped

115 g/4 oz pecan nuts, chopped

55 g/2 oz freshly grated Parmesan cheese

2 tbsp chopped fresh mixed herbs

2 tbsp wholemeal flour

2 tbsp sunflower oil, plus extra for oiling

salt and pepper

TO SERVE

burger buns

salad leaves

tomato slices

tomato ketchup

1. Cook the butternut squash in a saucepan of boiling water for 15—20 minutes, or until tender. Drain and finely chop or mash. Set aside.

2. Place the water in a separate saucepan and bring to the boil. Slowly pour in the polenta in a steady stream and cook over a gentle heat, stirring, for 5 minutes, or until thick.

3. Remove the saucepan from the heat and stir in the butternut squash, celeriac, spring onions, pecan nuts, cheese, herbs and salt and pepper to taste. Mix well, then shape into four to six burger patties. Coat the burgers in the flour, cover and leave to chill for 1 hour.

4. Prepare the barbecue and preheat to medium-hot.

5. Grease the barbecue grill. Lightly brush the burgers with the oil and cook for 5—6 minutes on each side, or until cooked through. Transfer to serving plates and serve immediately in the burger buns with the salad leaves, tomato slices and tomato ketchup.

THESE DELICIOUS VEGGIE BURGERS MAKE A GREAT ALTERNATIVE TO THE STANDARD BEAN BURGER.

Chapter 7
SIDES & SAUCES

Classic BBQ Sauce

☆ MAKES 900 ML/1½ PINTS ☆

PREP: 10 MINS

COOK: 50 MINS

INGREDIENTS

1 small onion

2 garlic cloves

1 tbsp olive oil

225 ml/8 fl oz tomato ketchup

450 ml/16 fl oz passata

100 g/3½ oz brown sugar

4 tbsp cider vinegar

2 tbsp Worcestershire sauce

½–1 tsp cayenne pepper

½–1 tsp smoked paprika or ground chipotle powder

1. Put the onion and garlic into a food processor and purée.

2. Heat the oil in a heavy-based frying pan over a medium-high heat. Add the onion-garlic purée and cook, stirring frequently, until it begins to brown.

3. Add the remaining ingredients and bring to the boil. Reduce the heat to medium and simmer for about 45 minutes, stirring occasionally, until the sauce thickens and begins to darken. Bottle quickly in sterilized bottles or jars and store in a cool place or refrigerator until required.

THIS CLASSIC SAUCE CAN BE
USED AS A CONDIMENT WITH ANY
MEAT DISH OR YOU CAN ALSO USE
IT TO MARINATE BEEF OR PORK
BEFORE GRILLING.

Home-made Tomato
Ketchup

☆ MAKES 250 ML/9 FL OZ ☆

PREP: 10 MINS

COOK: 15-20 MINS

INGREDIENTS

2 tbsp olive oil

1 red onion, chopped

2 garlic cloves, chopped

250 g/9 oz plum tomatoes, chopped

250 g/9 oz canned chopped tomatoes

½ tsp ground ginger

½ tsp chilli powder

40 g/1½ oz dark brown sugar

100 ml/3½ fl oz red wine vinegar

salt and pepper

1. Heat the olive oil in a large saucepan and add the onion, garlic and all of the tomatoes. Add the ginger and chilli and season with salt and pepper to taste. Cook for 15 minutes, or until soft.

2. Pour the mixture into a food processor or blender and blend well. Sieve thoroughly to remove all the seeds. Return the mixture to the pan and add the sugar and vinegar. Return to the boil and cook until it is the consistency of ketchup.

3. Bottle quickly in sterilized bottles or jars and store in a cool place or refrigerator until required.

THIS HOME-MADE VERSION OF THE TRADITIONAL SAUCE IS MUCH MORE FLAVOURSOME THAN SHOP BOUGHT.

Mayonnaise

 MAKES 300 ML/10 FL OZ

 PREP: 10 MINS

COOK: NO COOKING

INGREDIENTS

2 large egg yolks

2 tsp Dijon mustard

¾ tsp salt, or to taste

2 tbsp lemon juice or white wine vinegar, plus extra if needed

about 300 ml/10 fl oz sunflower oil

white pepper

1. Whizz the egg yolks with the Dijon mustard, salt and white pepper to taste in a food processor, blender or by hand. Add the lemon juice and whizz again.

2. With the motor still running, add the oil, drop by drop at first. When the sauce begins to thicken, the oil can then be added in a slow, steady stream. Taste and adjust the seasoning with extra salt, pepper and lemon juice if necessary. If the sauce seems too thick, slowly add 1 tablespoon of hot water or lemon juice.

3. Use at once or store in a sterilized and airtight container in the refrigerator for up to 1 week.

THIS RICH AND CREAMY MAYONNAISE IS THE PERFECT ACCOMPANIMENT TO ANY BURGER OR SANDWICH.

Chipotle Ketchup & Chipotle Mustard

☆ MAKES 225 ML/8 FL OZ ☆

PREP: 10 MINS

COOK: 3-10 MINS

INGREDIENTS

CHIPOTLE KETCHUP

225 ml/8 fl oz tomato ketchup

½ tsp Worcestershire sauce

½ tsp soft light brown sugar

1 tbsp fresh lemon juice, or to taste

1½ tsp chipotle powder, or to taste

1 tsp ground cumin

½ tsp ground turmeric

¼ tsp ground ginger

salt

CHIPOTLE MUSTARD

125 ml/4 fl oz Dijon mustard

1 tsp chipotle powder, or to taste

1. For the ketchup, combine all the ingredients with salt to taste in a small saucepan and place over a medium heat. Bring to a simmer and cook, stirring frequently, for 5 minutes, or until the ketchup is slightly thickened. Remove from the heat and cool. Transfer to a sterilized jar, cover, and refrigerate until ready to use.

2. To make the chipotle mustard, place the ingredients in a small bowl and stir to thoroughly combine. Transfer to a sterilized jar, cover, and refrigerate until ready to use.

THESE SAUCES ARE GREAT FOR ANY SPICE LOVERS WHO PREFER THEIR BARBECUE RECIPES TO HAVE A BIT OF A KICK TO THEM.

Roadhouse Steak Sauce

★ MAKES 350 ML/12 FL OZ ★

PREP: 10 MINS

COOK: 50 MINS

INGREDIENTS

400 g/14 oz canned chopped tomatoes

150 ml/5 fl oz beef stock

4 garlic cloves, chopped

1 red onion, finely chopped

175 g/6 oz raisins

4 tbsp Worcestershire sauce

1 tbsp beef extract or rich beef stock cube, crumbled

1 tbsp mustard powder, dissolved in 1 tbsp water

2 tbsp white wine vinegar

1 tbsp golden syrup

1 tbsp soft dark brown sugar

½ tsp cayenne pepper

finely grated zest of 1 orange

salt and pepper

1. Mix together all the ingredients with salt and pepper to taste in a heavy-based saucepan over a high heat, stirring to dissolve the golden syrup and sugar. Bring to the boil, then reduce the heat to very low and simmer, stirring freqently, for 30 minutes, or until the mixture is blended and the raisins are falling apart.

2. Transfer the mixture to a blender or food processor and purée. Strain the mixture through a fine sieve into the cleaned pan, rubbing backwards and forwards with a wooden spoon and scraping the base of the sieve to produce as much purée as possible.

3. Place the pan over a medium heat and bring the purée to the boil. Reduce the heat to medium-low and simmer, uncovered, for 15 minutes, or until the sauce has thickened and reduced. Transfer to a bowl and leave to cool completely. Adjust the salt and pepper to taste.

4. The sauce can be used immediately, or stored in a sterilized container in the refrigerator for up to 3 weeks.

Blistering Beer & Chilli Sauce

☆ MAKES 450 ML/16 FL OZ ☆

PREP: 10 MINS

COOK: 45 MINS

INGREDIENTS

2 tbsp sunflower oil

1 red onion, finely chopped

1 tbsp ancho chilli powder

1½ tsp cayenne pepper

250 g/9 oz tomato ketchup

4 tbsp treacle

2 tbsp soft dark brown sugar

2 tsp salt

¼ tsp pepper

325 ml/11 fl oz pale ale

2 tbsp cider vinegar or red wine vinegar

2 tbsp Worcestershire sauce

3 red, green or mixed jalapeño chillies, chopped

---

1. Heat the oil in a saucepan over a medium-high heat. Add the onion and fry for 3–5 minutes, or until soft. Add the chilli powder and cayenne pepper, then stir for 30 seconds. Add the remaining ingredients, except the chillies, stirring until the ketchup, treacle and sugar are blended.

2. Bring to the boil, skimming the surface, as necessary. Add the chillies. Reduce the heat and leave to gently bubble, skimming the surface as necessary and stirring occasionally, for about 30 minutes, or until the sauce has a coating consistency.

3. Transfer the sauce to a food processor or blender and purée. Pass the mixture through a sieve, rubbing backwards and forwards with a wooden spoon and scraping the base of the sieve to produce as much purée as possible.

4. The sauce can be used immediately or it can be left to cool completely and stored in an airtight container in the refrigerator for up to 2 weeks.

Celeriac, Fennel & Peach Slaw

SERVES 4   PREP: 10 mins   NO COOKING

INGREDIENTS

4 tbsp mayonnaise

1 tsp sriracha chilli sauce

1 tsp horseradish sauce

juice and zest of 1 lemon

½ tsp pepper

2 ripe peaches, stoned and sliced

200 g/7 oz celeriac, cut into matchsticks

1 fennel bulb, sliced

1 small red onion, sliced

1. In a large bowl, whisk together the mayonnaise, chilli sauce, horseradish sauce, lemon zest, lemon juice and pepper.

2. Add the peaches, celeriac, fennel and onion to the bowl.

3. Mix well to combine thoroughly and then serve immediately.

THIS SLAW WILL WORK WELL
WITH ANY STONED FRUIT AND
IS GREAT SERVED WITH PORK,
CHICKEN OR FISH.

Creamy Potato Salad

☆ SERVES 8 ☆

PREP: 15 MINS + CHILLING

COOK: 30 MINS

INGREDIENTS

1.25 kg/2 lb 12 oz waxy potatoes

125 ml/4 fl oz mayonnaise

50 ml/2 fl oz soured cream

90 ml/3 fl oz white wine vinegar

1 tsp wholegrain mustard

½ tsp dried dill

75 g/2¾ oz red onions, finely chopped

30 g/1 oz celery, finely chopped

4 tbsp chopped gherkins

40 g/1½ oz roasted red peppers, chopped

2 hard-boiled eggs, chopped (optional)

salt and pepper

1. Place the unpeeled potatoes in a saucepan and cover with water by a few inches. Add salt, bring to the boil over a high heat, then reduce the heat and simmer for 20—30 minutes, or until just tender.

2. Put the mayonnaise, soured cream, vinegar, mustard, dill, and salt and pepper to taste into a bowl and mix together.

3. Drain the potatoes and leave to cool slightly, then slip off the skins with your fingers or with a paring knife. Chop the potatoes into 1-cm/½-inch pieces and add to the dressing while still warm. Stir in the onion, celery, gherkins, peppers and egg, if using. Cover and chill for at least 2 hours or overnight.

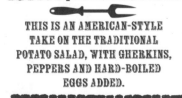

THIS IS AN AMERICAN-STYLE
TAKE ON THE TRADITIONAL
POTATO SALAD, WITH GHERKINS,
PEPPERS AND HARD-BOILED
EGGS ADDED.

Smoky BBQ Beans

☆ SERVES 4 ☆

PREP: 10 MINS

COOK: 30 MINS

INGREDIENTS

4 tbsp olive oil

1 large onion, chopped

2 garlic cloves, chopped

2 celery sticks, chopped

1 large carrot, chopped

1 tsp fennel seeds

2 tsp dried oregano

2 tsp smoked paprika

1 tbsp chipotle paste

1 tbsp treacle

450 ml/16 fl oz passata

400 g/14 oz canned
cannellini beans,
drained and rinsed

salt and pepper

1. Heat the oil in a large saucepan over a medium heat. Add the onion, garlic, celery and carrot and sweat with a lid on for 15 minutes, or until translucent and softened.

2. Add the fennel seeds, oregano, paprika, chipotle and treacle. Cook for 5 minutes to allow the sugars to start to caramelize.

3. Add the passata and beans and cook for a further 10 minutes.

4. Season to taste and serve.

FOR THE MEAT-LOVING
CARNIVORE, TRY ADDING
SMOKED BACON OR CHORIZO.

Buttermilk Burger Buns

PREP: 2½ HOURS

COOK: 10-20 MINS

INGREDIENTS

400 g/14 oz strong
bread flour

150 g/5½ oz plain flour,
plus extra for dusting

100 g/3½ oz
butter, diced

1 large egg

2 tbsp sugar

7 g/¼ oz dried yeast

300 ml/10 fl oz
buttermilk

1 tsp salt

1 lightly beaten egg,
to glaze

1. In a large bowl, mix together the flours and rub in the butter until it resembles fine breadcrumbs.

2. In a medium bowl, whisk together the egg, sugar, yeast, buttermilk and salt.

3. Pour the egg mixture into the bowl with the flour. Using the back of a wooden spoon, combine all the ingredients together. Tip the dough out onto a floured work surface and knead for 10 minutes, or until elastic and smooth.

4. Place the dough in a clean bowl, cover with clingfilm and leave in a warm place to rise for 1½ hours.

5. Once the dough has risen, knock back then tip onto a floured surface. Divide the mixture into 8 or 16 depending on whether you are making burger buns or slider buns. Roll into ball shapes and place onto a large baking tray, leaving enough space in between for the buns to double in size.

6. Cover the baking tray with clingfilm and leave in a warm place for 30–40 minutes, or until doubled in size. Preheat the oven to 180°C/350°F/Gas Mark 4.

7. Brush the buns lightly with the egg and bake in the preheated oven for 15–20 minutes for the large buns and 10–15 minutes for the smaller buns.

MAKING BREAD BY HAND IS
A GREAT WAY OF RELIEVING
STRESS.

Corn on the Cob
with Blue Cheese

☆ SERVES 6 ☆

PREP: 20 MINS

COOK: 15-20 MINS

INGREDIENTS

140 g/5 oz blue cheese

140 g/5 oz curd cheese

125 ml/4 fl oz natural Greek yogurt

6 corn cobs in their husks

salt and pepper

1. Prepare the barbecue for direct cooking and preheat to medium. Crumble the blue cheese into a bowl. Beat with a wooden spoon until creamy. Beat in the curd cheese until thoroughly blended. Gradually beat in the yogurt and season to taste with salt and pepper. Cover with clingfilm and leave to chill somewhere cool until required.

2. Fold back the husks on each corn cob and remove the silks. Smooth the husks back into place. Cut out 6 rectangles of double-thickness aluminium foil, each large enough to enclose a corn cob. Wrap the corn cobs in pieces of double-thickness aluminium foil.

3. Place the corn cobs on the barbecue grill and cook for 15–20 minutes, turning frequently. Unwrap the corn cobs and discard the foil. Peel back the husk on one side of each and trim off with a sharp knife. Transfer to serving plates and serve with the blue cheese mixture spooned on top.

IF YOU AREN'T A FAN OF BLUE CHEESE, YOU COULD REPLACE THIS WITH A SOFT GOAT'S CHEESE INSTEAD.

Creamed Spinach

☆ SERVES 4 ☆

PREP: 10 MINS

COOK: 15-20 MINS

INGREDIENTS

4 tbsp olive oil

1 large shallot, diced

2 garlic cloves, crushed

100 g/3½ oz smoked
bacon lardons

1 large carrot, diced

150 g/5½ oz
celeriac, diced

¼ tsp salt

1 tsp pepper

200 ml/7 fl oz
double cream

250 g/9 oz fresh spinach

1. Heat the oil in a large saucepan over a medium heat. Add the shallot, garlic, lardons, carrot and celeriac. Sweat the vegetables with a lid on for 10 minutes, or until softened, stirring every now and then.

2. Season with the salt and pepper. Add the double cream and simmer the mixture until it is reduced by half.

3. Meanwhile, bring a medium saucepan of water to the boil. Blanch the spinach for a few seconds, then drain and run under cold water until the spinach is cooled. Squeeze out the excess water from the spinach, then add to the creamed vegetables. Stir to combine and serve immediately.

FOR A HEALTHIER VERSION,
REPLACE THE DOUBLE CREAM
WITH LIGHT OR SOYA CREAM.

Garlic Bread

 SERVES 6

 PREP: 15 MINS

COOK: 10-15 MINS

INGREDIENTS

150 g/5½ oz butter, softened

3 garlic cloves, crushed

2 tbsp chopped fresh flat-leaf parsley

pepper

1 large or 2 small sticks of French bread

1. Prepare the barbecue for indirect cooking and preheat to medium-hot.

2. Mix the butter, garlic and parsley together in a bowl until well combined. Season to taste with pepper and mix well.

3. Make several lengthways cuts in the bread but be careful not to cut all the way through.

4. Spread the flavoured butter over one side of each cut and place the loaf on a large sheet of double-thickness aluminium foil.

5. Wrap the bread in the aluminium foil, place on the barbecue grill and cook for 10—15 minutes, or until the butter melts and the bread is piping hot. Serve immediately.

FOR AN ADDED TREAT, ADD SOME GRATED CHEESE TO THE CUTS IN THE BREAD AND COOK UNTIL MELTED.

Chapter 8
DRINKS

Fresh Lemonade

★ SERVES 6 ★

PREP: 15 MINS
+ STANDING

COOK: NO COOKING

INGREDIENTS

4 large lemons,
preferably unwaxed

175 g/6 oz caster sugar

900 ml/1½ pints boiling
water

ice cubes

1. Scrub the lemons well, then dry. Using a vegetable peeler, pare three of the lemons very thinly. Place the peel in a large jug or basin, add the sugar and boiling water and stir well until the sugar has dissolved. Cover the jug and leave to stand for at least 3 hours, stirring occasionally. Meanwhile, squeeze the juice from the three lemons and reserve.

2. Remove and discard the lemon peel and stir in the reserved lemon juice. Thinly slice the remaining lemon and cut the slices in half. Add to the lemonade together with the ice cubes. Stir and serve immediately.

YOU CAN TRY USING ORANGES OR LIMES OR ALL THREE FRUITS FOR SOME EQUALLY REFRESHING THIRST QUENCHERS.

Tips for Hosting an Amazing Barbecue

As summer days begin to heat up the air outside, you're probably starting to think about heating up the grill and inviting friends over to admire your grilling skills. With a bit of planning you can make it the event of the season.

1. Don't try to be a short-order cook. Keep the menu simple. Choose just three or four proteins at the most and do them well rather than trying to cook a million different things. Burgers (these can be beef, turkey, fish or veggie) or sausages, a beef dish, a chicken dish and a fish or veggie dish are usually enough to satisfy most crowds. There's plenty of inspiration in this book for making these dishes as exciting and tasty as possible.

2. Do all of your prep ahead of time. Before a single lick of fire touches your grill, make sure you've chopped, sliced, marinated and skewered everything you plan to put on the grill.

3. Put drinks on ice. Fill a large bucket or cooler with ice and stock it with beer, soft drinks, wine and cider before your guests arrive. If you have a co-host who is willing to take charge of the drinks, offer home-made cocktails, punch, iced tea, etc. If you want to fancy up your drinks, offer ice cubes with chunks of fruit or whole berries frozen in them.

4. Don't forget the condiments. For many, a burger's just not a burger if it's not dripping with sweet-salty-spicy sauces and loaded up with veggies. If you're serving hamburgers (or sausages) create a condiment station and set out an assortment of mustards, ketchups, relishes, pickled veggies, crunchy lettuce, sliced tomatoes, fresh herbs, chillies, and bacon and let guests choose their own accompaniments.

5. Serve make-ahead or store-bought appetizers. Don't make hungry guests stand around while you wait for the coals to get hot or that giant roast to cook through. Set out chips and salsa, assorted crudités with a bowl of creamy dip, or a cheese and cracker spread for people to nosh on while they take in your barbecuing prowess.

Sweet Iced Tea

☆ SERVES 2 ☆

PREP: 15 MINS
+ CHILLING

COOK:
5 MINS

INGREDIENTS

300 ml/10 fl oz water

2 tea bags

100 ml/3½ fl oz
orange juice

4 tbsp lime juice

1-2 tbsp brown sugar

ice cubes

TO DECORATE

1 lime wedge

granulated sugar

orange or lime slices

1. Pour the water into a saucepan and bring to the boil. Remove from the heat, add the tea bags and leave to infuse for 5 minutes. Remove the tea bags and leave the tea to cool to room temperature. Transfer to a jug, cover with clingfilm and chill in the refrigerator for at least 45 minutes.

2. When the tea has chilled, pour in the orange juice and lime juice. Add sugar to taste.

3. Take two glasses and rub the rims with the lime wedge, then dip them in granulated sugar to frost. Put the ice cubes into the glasses and pour over the tea. Decorate with orange or lime slices and serve immediately.

AT SUMMER PARTIES, PLACE
BUCKETS FILLED WITH ICE
CUBES AT VARIOUS POINTS SO
GUESTS CAN HELP THEMSELVES.

Cookie Dough & Caramel
Cola Float

★ SERVES 4 ★

PREP: 25 MINS
+ RESTING
+ FREEZING

COOK:
20 MINS

INGREDIENTS

COOKIE DOUGH ICE CREAM

55 g/2 oz
butter, softened

30 g/1 oz soft light
brown sugar

30 g/1 oz dark
brown sugar

2 tsp vanilla extract

85 g/3 oz plain flour

55 g/2 oz plain
chocolate chips

225 ml/8 fl oz whole milk

6 egg yolks

150 g/5½ oz caster sugar

225 ml/8 fl oz
double cream

150 ml/5 fl oz
caramel syrup

1 litre/1¾ pints cola

1. In a food processor, beat together the butter and brown sugars for about 4 minutes, until pale. Add 1 tsp of vanilla and the flour and then pulse until it starts to come together. Turn out onto a board and fold in the chocolate chips by hand.

2. Wrap the dough in clingfilm and leave in the refrigerator for 30 minutes to rest.

3. Meanwhile, slowly heat the milk in a medium saucepan. In a heatproof bowl, whisk together the egg yolks, the remaining vanilla and the caster sugar. When the milk comes to the boil, remove from the heat and pour slowly into the egg mixture, whisking as you pour. Pour back into a clean saucepan and slowly heat, stirring with a wooden spoon. Do not let it boil. Remove from the heat when the sauce has thickened, then add the double cream and leave to cool slightly before putting into an ice-cream machine. Churn until almost frozen.

4. Remove the cookie dough from the refrigerator and break into walnut-sized pieces. Add the pieces to the ice cream. Allow to churn a couple of times to mix into the dough without breaking up the pieces too much. Transfer to a freezer container and freeze for an hour, or until required.

5. Scoop the ice cream into four tall glasses. Pour over the caramel and top with cola.

IF YOU HAVE NOT GOT THE TIME
OR AN ICE-CREAM MACHINE,
DON'T FEEL BAD ABOUT USING
SHOP-BOUGHT ICE CREAM.

Spicy Bourbon Pickleback

✫ SERVES 1 ✫

PREP: 1 MIN

NO COOKING

INGREDIENTS

25 ml/1 oz bourbon

25 ml/1 oz brine from a jalapeño pickle jar

1. Place the bourbon and brine in two separate shot glasses.

2. Knock back the bourbon.

3. Then drink the pickle juice in one shot as a chaser!

TRY USING DIFFERENT PICKLE JUICES, SUCH AS OLIVES, GHERKINS, CABBAGE, PICKLED ONIONS OR EVEN PICKLED EGGS.

Club Mojito

☆ SERVES 1 ☆

PREP: 5 MINS

NO COOKING

INGREDIENTS

1 tsp sugar syrup

6 fresh mint leaves, plus extra to decorate

juice of ½ lime

4–6 cracked ice cubes

50 ml/2 fl oz Jamaican rum

soda water

dash Angostura bitters

1. Put the sugar syrup, mint leaves and lime juice into a tumbler or small glass.

2. Muddle the mint leaves, then add the cracked ice cubes and the rum.

3. Top up with soda water.

4. Finish with the Angostura bitters and decorate with the remaining mint leaves.

5. Serve immediately.

THIS FRESH AND FRUITY DRINK GOES DOWN A TREAT ON A HOT SUMMER'S DAY.

Sangria

☆ **SERVES 6** ☆

PREP: 10 MINS + MARINATING

COOK: NO COOKING

INGREDIENTS

juice of 1 orange

juice of 1 lemon

2 tbsp icing sugar

cracked ice

1 orange, thinly sliced

1 lemon, thinly sliced

1 bottle chilled red wine

lemonade, to taste

1. Put the orange juice and lemon juice in a large jug. Stir.

2. Add the sugar and stir. When the sugar has dissolved, add 4–6 cracked ice cubes.

3. Add the sliced fruit and the wine and marinate for 1 hour.

4. Add lemonade to taste, then top up with cracked ice.

5. Serve immediately.

THIS IS A GREAT COCKTAIL TO SERVE WHEN GUESTS ARRIVE AT THE BARBECUE.

Whiskey Sling

SERVES 1

PREP: 5 MINS

COOK: NO COOKING

INGREDIENTS

1 tsp icing sugar

25 ml/1 fl oz lemon juice

1 tsp water

50 ml/2 fl oz American blended whiskey

cracked ice

1 orange wedge

1. Put the sugar into a glass.

2. Add the lemon juice and water and stir until the sugar has dissolved.

3. Pour in the whiskey and stir to mix.

4. Half-fill a small, chilled tumbler with cracked ice and strain the cocktail over it. Decorate with the orange wedge.

5. Serve immediately.

THIS IS AN IDEAL END OF THE NIGHT COCKTAIL FOR ALL WHISKEY LOVERS.

Port & Stout Cocktail

★ SERVES 2 ★

PREP: 5 MINS

COOK: NO COOKING

INGREDIENTS

25 ml/1 fl oz port

150 ml/5 fl oz stout

200 ml/7 fl oz ginger beer

dash of orange Angostura bitters

ice cubes

1. Pour the port, stout, ginger beer and bitters into a cocktail shaker.

2. Top with ice cubes, put the lid on and shake the cocktail vigorously.

3. Pour over ice into two glasses and serve.

THIS RECIPE MAKES A GREAT PUNCH. JUST INCREASE THE QUANTITIES AND ADD A FEW ORANGE SLICES.

Salty Dog

☆ SERVES 1 ☆

PREP: 5 MINS

COOK: NO COOKING

INGREDIENTS

1 tbsp granulated sugar

1 tbsp coarse salt

1 lime wedge

cracked ice cubes

50 ml/2 fl oz vodka

grapefruit juice, to taste

1. Mix the sugar and salt in a saucer.

2. Rub the rim of a chilled cocktail glass with the lime wedge.

3. Dip into the sugar and salt mixture, to coat.

4. Fill the glass with cracked ice cubes and pour over the vodka. Top up with the grapefruit juice and stir.

5. Serve immediately.

THE SHARP FLAVOURS OF THE GRAPEFRUIT JUICE AND VODKA COMBINE BEAUTIFULLY WITH THE SUGAR AND SALT.

Chapter 9
DESSERTS

Grilled Bourbon Peaches

SERVES 4

PREP: 15 MINS

COOK: 20 MINS

INGREDIENTS

6 ripe peaches, stoned and halved

1 tbsp oil

4 tbsp good-quality bourbon

100 g/3½ oz butter

150 g/5½ oz dark brown sugar

1 tsp vanilla extract

150 ml/5 fl oz apple juice

vanilla ice cream, to serve

1. Prepare the barbecue for direct cooking and preheat to hot.

2. Brush the flesh side of the peach halves with the oil.

3. In a saucepan over a high heat, flambé the bourbon then add the butter, sugar, vanilla and apple juice. Bring to a simmer and let everything dissolve and turn slightly syrupy. Remove from the heat and leave to cool.

4. Lay the peaches, skin-side down, on the barbecue grill and cook for 2 minutes, or until the skin starts to char. Carefully turn over with a palette knife and cook for a further 2 minutes.

5. Remove the peaches from the barbecue and serve with ice cream and the bourbon syrup.

TRY THIS RECIPE WITH
A MIXTURE OF STONE FRUIT
AND USE RUM INSTEAD
OF BOURBON.

Chocolate & Rum Bananas

PREP: 15 MINS

COOK: 5-10 MINS

INGREDIENTS

1 tbsp melted butter

225 g/8 oz plain or milk chocolate

4 large bananas

2 tbsp rum

mascarpone cheese, to serve

1. Prepare the barbecue for direct cooking and preheat to medium. Take four large squares of double-thickness aluminium foil and brush them with the butter.

2. Cut the chocolate into very small pieces. Carefully make a slit, lengthways, in the peel of each banana, and open just wide enough to insert the chocolate. Place the chocolate pieces inside the bananas, along their lengths, then close them up.

3. Wrap each stuffed banana in a square of foil. Place on the barbecue grill and cook for 5–10 minutes, or until the chocolate has melted. Remove from the heat, place the bananas on plates and pour some rum into each banana.

4. Serve immediately with mascarpone cheese.

FOR CHILDREN, PLEASE JUST OMIT THE RUM AND INSTEAD SERVE WITH MARSHMALLOWS AND ICE CREAM.

Choosing the Right Smoking Wood

MILD

For mild smoke flavour, choose alder or fruit woods like apple or cherry. They'll impart a mild smokiness with a hint of fruity sweetness. These are great choices for smoking more delicate foods like poultry or fish. Alder is especially mild with a hint of sweetness. Apple and cherry offer fruity notes and go well with either chicken or pork.

MEDIUM

For a medium smoke flavour, oak, hickory or maple are your best bets. They'll impart a distinctive and intense smokiness without overpowering the meat. These are great choices for poultry, pork or beef. Hickory is probably the most common smoking wood. Its flavour is intense so it is often mixed with a milder wood to tone it down. Oak offers a milder smokiness than hickory and a bit more flavour than apple or cherry making it a good wood to mix with hickory.

HEAVY

Mesquite, the smokiest of all the smoking woods, is what is typically used for Texas-style barbecue. That's because hearty meats like brisket can hold their own against the intense smoke flavour it delivers. Used sparingly, in combination with milder woods, it can be used successfully for fish, chicken, pork or beef.

Banana & Chocolate
S'mores

SERVES 4

PREP: 15 MINS

COOK: 10-15 MINS

INGREDIENTS

8 marshmallows

8 chocolate chip cookies

1 banana, thinly sliced

4 squares dark chocolate

1. Prepare the barbecue for direct cooking and preheat to medium.

2. Thread two of the marshmallows onto pre-soaked wooden skewers or metal skewers. Toast over the barbecue until they soften.

3. Place the toasted marshmallows on top of a cookie, top with a few slices of banana and a square of chocolate, and sandwich together with another cookie. Repeat with the remaining cookies, marshmallows and other ingredients. Serve each s'more while they are still hot.

THIS IS A TWIST ON THE CLASSIC AMERICAN CAMPFIRE DESSERT, THE S'MORE. THIS VERSION USES CHOCOLATE CHIP COOKIES.

Boozy Nectarines

 SERVES 4

 PREP: 15 MINS · COOK: 15-20 MINS

INGREDIENTS

8 ripe nectarines

50 g/1¾ oz butter, plus extra for greasing

3 tbsp demerara sugar

amaretto liqueur

vanilla ice cream, to serve

1. Prepare the barbecue for direct cooking and preheat to medium-low. Brush eight pieces of double-thickness aluminium foil with butter.

2. Place a nectarine on each square of foil. Top with a small knob of butter, a sprinkle of sugar, and a few drops of the amaretto liqueur. Wrap the foil into a loose parcel, sealing well.

3. Place on the barbecue grill and cook, with the lid on, for 15–20 minutes, or until tender. Serve immediately with ice cream.

THESE BOOZY NECTARINES ALSO
WORK WELL WITH COGNAC OR
BRANDY.

Fruit Skewers

 SERVES 4

PREP: 15 MINS

COOK: 5–10 MINS

INGREDIENTS

a selection of fruit, such as apricots, peaches, strawberries, mangoes, pineapple and bananas, prepared and cut into chunks

2 tbsp maple syrup, plus extra for drizzling

50 g/1¾ oz plain chocolate (optional)

1. Prepare the barbecue for direct cooking and preheat to medium-hot.

2. Thread alternate pieces of fruit onto four pre-soaked wooden skewers or metal skewers. Brush the fruit with the maple syrup.

3. Put the chocolate, if using, in a heatproof bowl. Set the bowl over a saucepan of barely simmering water and stir until the chocolate has completely melted.

4. Place the skewers on the barbecue grill and cook for 3 minutes, or until caramelized. Transfer to serving plates and serve immediately, drizzled with the melted chocolate, if using, and maple syrup.

THESE SKEWERS COULD ALSO BE
SERVED WITH LOW-FAT FROMAGE
FRAIS, RATHER THAN THE
MELTED CHOCOLATE.

Caramelized Apple Rings

 SERVES 4

PREP: 15 MINS

 COOK: 5–6 MINS

INGREDIENTS

4 crisp apples, such as Braeburn

juice of ½ lemon

3 tbsp demerara sugar

¼ tsp ground cinnamon

25 g/1 oz melted butter, plus extra for oiling

vanilla ice cream or clotted cream, to serve

1. Prepare the barbecue for direct cooking and preheat to hot.

2. Remove and discard a thin slice from the top and bottom of the apples. Remove the cores and slice each apple into 3 thick rings. Place in a bowl and toss with the lemon juice to prevent discoloration.

3. Mix the sugar and cinnamon and sprinkle over the apples, tossing thoroughly to coat. Brush with some of the melted butter. Reserve any liquid in a bowl.

4. Brush the grill with butter. Place the apples on the barbecue grill and cook for 5–6 minutes, or until golden and slightly charred, turning every 2 minutes and brushing with butter and the reserved liquid. Transfer to serving bowls and serve immediately with ice cream.

INDEX

INDEX